A Chaldean map of the world, from a drawing by Faucher-Gudin in
Maspero's Dawn of Civilization

THE WORLD'S GREAT EXPLORERS

Explorers of the Ancient World

By Charnan Simon

 CHILDRENS PRESS ®

CHICAGO

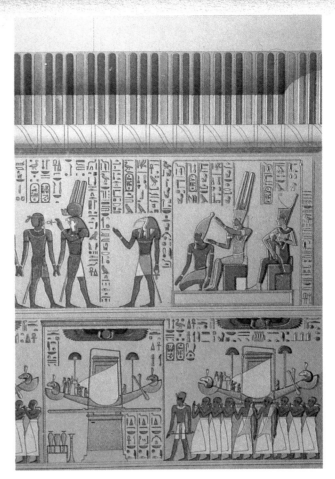

Bas-relief in the granite chambers at Karnak, an Egyptian town on the banks of the Nile

Project Editor: Ann Heinrichs
Designer: Lindaanne Donohoe
Typesetter: Compositors Corporation
Engraver: Liberty Photoengraving

**Library of Congress
Cataloging-in-Publication Data**
Simon, Charnan.
   Explorers of the ancient world /
Charnan Simon.
      p.   cm. — (The World's great
explorers)
   Summary: Brief biographies
emphasizing the voyages and discoveries
of various explorers of the ancient world
including Hanno of Carthage, Nehsi of
Egypt, Pytheas of Greece, and Alexander
the Great.
   Includes bibliographical references.
   ISBN 0-516-03053-1
   1. Explorers—Juvenile literature. 2.
Discoveries (in geography)—Juvenile
literature. [1. Explorers. 2. Discoveries
(in geography)] I. Title. II. Series.
G175.S5 1990
910.92—dc20
[B]
[920]   89-25431
                                CIP
                                AC

The siege of Tyre, capital of ancient Phoenicia

Table of Contents

Chapter 1
"Neither Wise Men
Nor Foolish"

The day dawned fair and bright in Carthage. The blue Mediterranean Sea sparkled in the sunlight, and a brisk breeze blew up from the harbor. Outside the walls of this prosperous North African city, slaves were busy tending the wheat fields owned by their Phoenician masters. Within the city walls, craftsmen were busy, too. Weavers, glass-makers, perfume makers, potters, jewelers, ivory carvers—all were hard at work fashioning the items for which they were famous throughout the world.

In 500 B.C., the "world" did not extend very far. Almost all that the Phoenicians knew of the world were the lands around the Mediterranean Sea. The outer limits of that world were the Pillars of Hercules to the west, the Red Sea to the south, the Black Sea to the north, and a glimpse of Arabia and Persia to the east. Even at that, the Phoenicians knew more than most of their neighbors did, for they were traders and sailors. Phoenician merchant ships had explored virtually every corner of the Mediterranean. Their goods were prized in cities from Spain to Persia.

Ships of the Phoenician mariners

For years the Phoenicians had been the undisputed masters of the Mediterranean. Now, however, Greeks were crowding in on Phoenician territory. Greek traders were competing with Phoenician merchants. The Mediterranean was getting too small for the people of Carthage!

The Phoenicians living in Carthage decided to move on. If there was too much competition in the old markets, they would find new markets. They would outwit the Greeks by going beyond the Mediterranean. They would establish new trading centers where the Greeks would never dare to follow.

Around 500 B.C., the Phoenicians outfitted two expeditions. One of them, led by a man named Himilco, sailed west through the Pillars of Hercules (today's Strait of Gibraltar) and then north into the Atlantic. Not much is known about this journey. The Roman historian Pliny wrote a few lines about it in the first century A.D., some five hundred years after Himilco's voyage. And the Roman poet Avienus, who lived another four hundred years after Pliny, put Himilco in one of his poems. This was almost a thousand years after the Carthaginian's actual voyage!

These accounts do not exactly provide an accurate, precise travelog. But from these two sources, sketchy as they are, it appears that Himilco set out with a fleet of as many as sixty ships. He cruised in the Atlantic for four months, exploring the coasts of Spain and France, possibly even reaching Britain. But he was never able to establish colonies or trading centers, and his reports of the area discouraged other curious sailors.

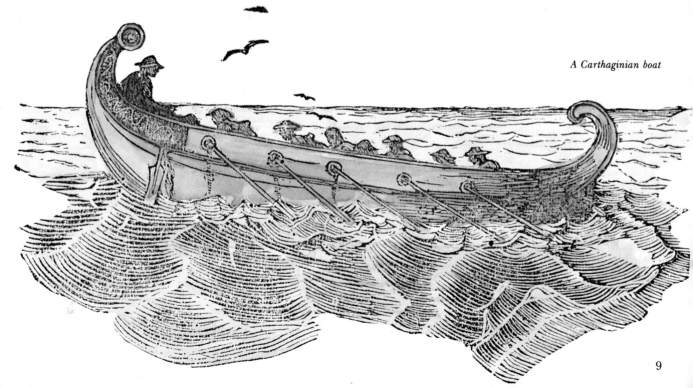

A Carthaginian boat

As Avienus tells it: "Himilco relates . . . that none have sailed over these waters, because propelling winds are lacking . . . and because darkness screens the light of day with a sort of clothing, and because a fog always conceals the sea . . . there is much seaweed among the waves, that keeps vessels back as brush delays a man in walking . . . the sea has no great depth, and the surface of the earth is barely covered by a little water. The monsters of the sea move continually hither and thither, and the wild beasts swim among the sluggish and slowly creeping ships."

If Avienus was right, and this is truly what Himilco reported, it is no wonder that later explorers were discouraged from heading out into the Atlantic!

The second expedition from Carthage was more fortunate. It was led by a man named Hanno, who was said to be Himilco's brother. Instead of going north into the Atlantic, Hanno headed south after passing the Pillars of Hercules. When he returned home to Carthage, he had the story of his voyage carved on a stone tablet (there were no books in those days). The tablet itself has long since been lost, but a Greek translation of the story has survived.

Hanno's story begins simply enough. One fine morning in Carthage some 2,500 years ago, "It pleased the Carthaginians to commission Hanno to go seafaring beyond the Pillars of Hercules and there to found Libyo-Phoenician settlements."

But the scene at the Carthage harbor was probably not as simple. Some sixty ships were outfitted for the trip. The ships were huge, with curved wooden keels and large, square sails dyed the famous Tyrian purple. Each ship was manned by fifty oarsmen and had a hold big enough to carry provisions for the journey, as well

Hanno, the great Carthaginian mariner, sailing the western coast of Africa

for establishing permanent colonies along the route. All in all, there were said to be some thirty thousand men and women on board the fleet!

At last the word came to set sail. Farmers, carpenters, craftsmen, and sailors crowded the decks as the sails caught the wind. Slowly, surely, the great fleet headed westward out of the Carthage harbor.

The first segment of the journey was literally a breeze. Phoenician sailors had mastered the Mediterranean waters hundreds of years earlier. This great tideless sea, with its predictable winds, clear starlit nights, and familiar landmarks, offered no real challenge to Hanno's sea captains.

But once the ships passed beyond the Pillars of Hercules, things changed. Throughout history, this was as far as ancient peoples had dared to sail. A Greek poet of the time described the Strait of Gibraltar as "the Pillars of Hercules/Beyond which may travel neither wise men nor foolish."

Hanno and his sailors nevertheless traveled on into the uncharted Atlantic. They had no compasses to guide them—nothing, in fact, except the sun, the stars, and their own instincts. Hugging the west African coastline, they took to their oars when the wind was against them and unfurled the sails when the wind came up from behind.

Two days past the Pillars of Hercules, the fleet put to shore. There they founded their first colony, "which we named Thymaterium" (now Kenitra, Morocco). Leaving behind a group of settlers, along with provisions and one or two boats, the rest of the fleet pushed on. Their next stop was in a heavily forested area. No colony would be established here, but workers were left to erect a temple to the sea god, Poseidon.

Poseidon, god of the sea

The ships continued their southward way. Other colonies were founded, "called Cariconticos and Gytte, Acra and Melita, and Arambys." At one point the voyagers passed a large lake, "lying far from the sea and filled with abundance of large reeds. There elephants and a great number of other wild beasts were feeding."

At one point, the fleet put to shore and found friendly shepherds tending their flocks. Called Lixites, these shepherds told Hanno of the "inhospitable Ethiopians" who lived farther on. Their mountains were filled with wild beasts, said the Lixites, and with "a freakish race of men who run faster than horses."

When Hanno set sail again, several of the Lixite shepherds came with him to serve as interpreters. On they pushed, past two days of "desolate desert land" (the Sahara), to a small island where they founded a colony called Cerne. It is believed that Cerne was off the coast of present-day Western Sahara.

Cerne was to be the last of the Carthaginian colonies. From there on, Hanno's voyage became a nightmare. For years, Phoenician sailors had spread misleading and frightening tales to discourage other sailors from exploring their trade routes. Muddy seas, sharp rocks, and swirling whirlpools, bloodthirsty sea serpents, skydiving dragons—no detail was too horrible for the Phoenicians to include. Now it was as if some of their own horror stories were coming true to haunt them.

First there were the mountains, "peopled by swarms of wild men dressed in wild beasts' skins, who drove us off with stones and would not let us land." Sailing on, Hanno's ships next came to a river "large and broad, which was infested with crocodiles and river-horses [hippopotamuses]." It is now believed that this was the Senegal River.

For twelve more days the Carthaginians headed south. The only inhabitants they met were Ethiopians "who would not wait our approval, but fled from us." (At that time, natives of central Africa were referred to as Ethiopians.) They sailed on past a sweet-smelling forest, and then a low-lying plain, where the travelers could see "fires flaring up by night in every quarter."

Finally Hanno reached a large bay, in the middle of which lay a large island. There was a great salt lake in the middle of this island—and in the middle of the lake was yet another, smaller island. There the travelers put ashore for fresh food and water. (Historians believe this island is in Bijagos Bay in today's Guinea-Bissau.)

A frightful sea serpent, as drawn by Hans Egidius

They did not stay long. In the middle of the night they were awakened to find fires burning and chaos raging everywhere. According to Hanno's account, "We heard the noise of pipes and cymbals and the din of tom-toms and confused shouts. We were seized with a great fear, and our interpreters told us to abandon the island."

Hanno's narrative assures us that the fleet lost no time is doing just that. But even more terrors lay ahead of them: "We passed a country burning with fires and perfumes and streams of fire supplied from it fell into the sea. The country was impassable from the heat. So we sailed away in terror, and passing on for four days, we discovered at night a country full of fire. In the center a leaping blaze towered above the others and ap-

The voyagers being pelted with stones

peared to reach the stars. This was the highest mountain which we saw: it was called the Chariot of the Gods."

By now Hanno and his sailors were getting discouraged. Still, they pushed onward until they reached another large bay, now thought to be off the coast of Sierra Leone. Again there was an island in this bay—again the ships put to shore—and again they had an unpleasant surprise. As Hanno put it, "The island was filled with wild people. By far the greater number were women with hairy bodies. Our interpreters called them Gorillas. We gave chase but could not catch any of the men, for they all escaped up steep rocks and pelted us with stones. Three women were taken, but they attacked their captors with their teeth and hands, and could not be prevailed upon to accompany us."

Hanno's encounter with a "gorilla" of Sierra Leone

Not knowing what else to do, the Carthaginians killed and skinned these "women"—which were probably chimpanzees, and not humans, or even gorillas, at all.

It was an inglorious ending to a glorious adventure. The next words in Hanno's narrative are brief and to the point: "We did not sail further on, having run out of provisions."

And so Hanno returned to Carthage. It had been a remarkable voyage. Most historians agree that Hanno traveled at least as far as the coast of Sierra Leone. This means that his remarkable voyage had covered some 3,000 miles (4,828 kilometers)! Without maps or motors or compasses—with just a single sail and fifty able seamen per boat—Hanno's fleet had gone from the Medi-

The seacoast of ancient Carthage

terranean to within ten compass degrees of the equator. It was an amazing accomplishment.

Unfortunately, nothing really came of Hanno's discoveries. Carthaginian merchants did begin trading with the new cities just beyond the Pillars of Hercules. Probably they traded as far south as Hanno's colony of Cerne. But it was not until the fifteenth century, nearly two thousand years later, that seamen again sailed their ships as far south as Hanno had. These mariners were aided by compasses, sextants, and boats that sailed against the wind as well as with it. The fact remains that, in the history of exploration, Hanno the Navigator stands out as a true adventurer—as brave and intrepid a seaman as any that ever set sail.

Chapter 2
"With Marvels of the Land of Punt"

Hanno may be among the best known of all ancient explorers. But he certainly was not the only one, nor was he even the first. As long as there have been people on earth, there have been explorers.

Primitive people roamed far and wide in search of the roots, berries, and animals they needed for survival. Later, when people started raising their own food, communities spread out along the fertile river valleys that provided the best farmland. Tribes that raised animals were often nomadic, sometimes traveling hundreds of miles to find good grazing lands for their herds.

We know very little about these prehistoric explorers. This is because these people had not yet developed a system of writing. Stories of exploration and discovery began to emerge only after people began keeping written records of their activities. The presence of written records marks the beginning of what we call "historic" times. Earlier times are what we call "prehistoric."

Prehistoric tool-making

Up until about six thousand years ago, most people lived in small agricultural villages or were members of nomadic tribes. They lived this way all over the world—in Asia and Africa, in the Americas, in Europe, and in Australia and the Polynesian Islands.

Then things changed, at least in some places. People began to build cities along the richest river valleys. They learned to read and write, to barter goods, and to specialize in a particular job or craft. Instead of being farmers or herders, people did different things. They no longer grew their own food, made their own shoes, or built their own houses. Once living as self-sufficient farmers, people became city dwellers, dependent on one another for the necessities of life. They became what we now call civilized.

As far as we know, civilization began in the valleys of the Nile River in Egypt and the Tigris and Euphrates rivers in Mesopotamia (now Iraq). These lands, near the eastern end of the Mediterranean Sea, were bounteous. The climate was mild, the soil was rich, and there were plenty of natural resources. No one knows which of these civilizations arose first. We do know, however, that they used their rivers for transportation and that the two were in contact with each other.

Not much is known about early Mesopotamian explorers. Merchants shipped their wares up and down the Tigris and Euphrates rivers to the Persian Gulf. Sometimes they even ventured along the shores of the Arabian Sea toward India. But we have no surviving records of specific journeys of exploration that these people may have taken.

The meeting point of the Tigris and Euphrates rivers at al-Qurna, Iraq

The Egyptians are a different story. Archaeologists—scientists who study the far distant past—have found clues indicating that Egyptians were sailing up and down the Nile as early as ten thousand years ago. At first the Egyptians used boats made from tightly woven reeds of the papyrus plant. Later, they found that they needed larger, heavier, more seaworthy boats. To build these ships, they began importing fir, spruce, and cedar wood from other countries.

Why did the Egyptians need heavier boats? By about 5000 B.C., the people along the Nile were united into one great nation. Their ruler was called a Pharaoh, and the Egyptian people believed this Pharaoh to be half-man, half-god. Naturally, such a ruler could not be expected to live like a mere mortal. So the Pharaohs lived lives of great luxury. Their palaces and temples were huge, filled with priceless goods from other lands.

A Pharaoh's shopping list sounds as exotic today as it must have seemed to ordinary Egyptians five thousand years ago: turquoise and lapis lazuli, malachite and ivory; marble and polished granite; gold, silver, and copper; the feathers of exotic birds and skins of strange wild beasts; cedar and fir and spruce; incense and myrrh, spices, resins, and sweet-smelling herbs. The list goes on and on.

The Egyptians were not only interested in magnificence in this lifetime. They also believed in a life after death, and they wanted to live well there, too. When a Pharaoh died, his body was embalmed and wrapped in linen. The specially preserved body, called a mummy, was then placed in a decorated coffin and buried in a huge tomb. Along with it were placed the jewels, gold, and other priceless objects that he would need in the afterworld.

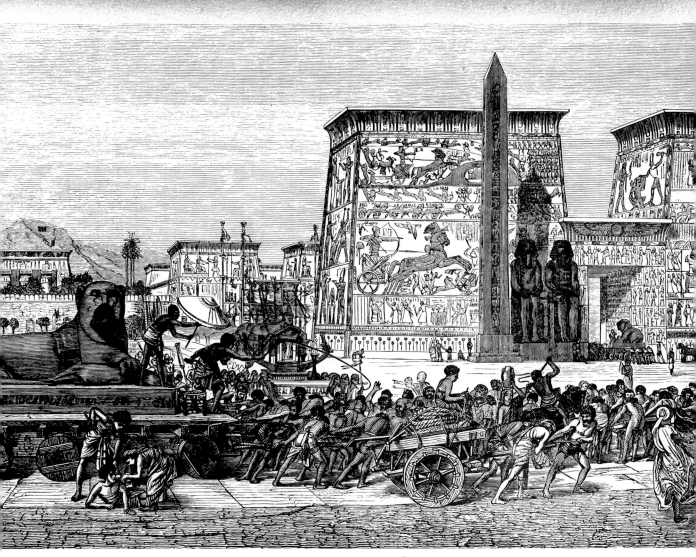

Laborers erecting public buildings in ancient Egypt

Many of the Pharaohs' tombs were Egypt's huge stone pyramids, still considered among the great wonders of the world. These pyramids were meant to be staircases by which the mummified Pharaohs could climb to the afterworld realm of the sun-god. Building them was no easy matter. Huge stones were brought long distances down the Nile by ferry; decorations and furnishings had to be imported from lands around the Mediterranean. The Egyptians used hundreds of slaves to build the pyramids. Records kept by the Egyptians show that many overseas trips were made to obtain these slaves.

Egyptian art made during the reign of Snefru

But what do we know of the actual voyages? The Egyptians' earliest recorded sea journey took place under a Pharaoh named Snefru, about 2600 B.C. According to Egyptian records, Snefru built sixty of his own boats and imported another forty made of cedar wood from Phoenicia. (Ancient Phoenicia is located near present-day Lebanon.) This means Snefru's ships had to leave the familiar banks of the Nile and venture out into the Mediterranean Sea.

Some two hundred years later, around 2400 B.C., we find another clue about Egyptian sea voyages. This clue was carved onto the walls of a temple built by the Pharaoh Sahure. Like Snefru, Sahure was a great shipbuilder. His temple carvings tell the story of how he, too, sent a fleet—eight ships this time—into the Mediterranean. But unlike Snefru, Sahure was looking for slaves, not wood for more ships.

Up until this time, no explorers were mentioned by name. Only the names of their Pharaohs were recorded. But around 2400 B.C., an Egyptian named Hannu became the world's first known explorer.

Hannu lived during the reign of the same King Sahure who sent out the slaving expedition. Hannu commanded another expedition sent out by Sahure—this time to a place called the Land of Punt.

Egyptians regarded the Land of Punt with awe. It was rich in gold, ivory, and exotic spices, and with the incense and myrrh the Egyptians used to embalm their dead. Many legends grew up about this fabulous place. Incense trees were guarded by giant serpents. Cinnamon was found in the nests of fierce eagles and could only be obtained at great hazard. There were leopards and wild apes and amazing dancing dwarfs. Some Egyptians even called Punt the Land of God.

Above: A home built on piles in the legendary Land of Punt
Below: The queen of Punt

25

No one today is exactly sure where Punt was located. Most scholars agree it was probably near present-day Somalia, the easternmost tip of Africa that juts out into the Indian Ocean.

In any case, though goods from Punt were being sent to Egypt before 2400 B.C., no Egyptian had ever traveled there before Hannu. Hannu knew what an important journey he was undertaking. When he returned to Egypt, he made sure that the story of his expedition was recorded on a stone. Over the centuries, this storytelling stone was buried deep in Egypt's sands. Only recently was the stone uncovered and the tale revealed.

As Hannu tells it, the expedition was organized "to fetch for Pharaoh sweet-smelling spices such as the princes of the red land collect out of fear and dread, such as he inspires in all nations." Hannu began his journey in the town of Hammamat, near the Nile River. Traveling by camel caravan, he made his way over the desert to the northern end of the Red Sea. There the expedition halted to build oceangoing ships.

Finally Hannu and his men were ready to sail down the Red Sea. Their ships would seem crude by today's standards, but they served the ancient Egyptians for centuries. Each ship had a large, flat hull and a single sail that could be used only when the ship was sailing with the wind. When the wind was against them, rows of standing oarsmen took over.

We do not know the details about Hannu's actual sea voyage. Without a map or compass, he was guided by the sun by day and the stars by night. Yet somehow he made his way along the coast of Africa to the fabled Land of Punt. His stone concludes by telling us that he was successful in loading his ships with treasure and returning home safely.

Ancient Egyptian ships

  Now our story skips ahead some nine hundred years to the next recorded journey to the Land of Punt.

  This voyage took place around 1500 B.C., during the reign of the beautiful and powerful Queen Hatshepsut. Egypt flourished during Queen Hatshepsut's reign. There were no wars, and the kingdom grew rich with trade. The queen took advantage of this peaceful, prosperous time to beautify her kingdom with new monuments and temples. One of her most famous buildings was the temple to the god Amon-Ra at Deir al-Bahri. Ruins of this temple still stand today. On its walls we find a remarkable series of carvings. They tell the story of an expedition Hatshepsut ordered to the fabled Land of Punt.

Queen Hatshepsut

The story is as follows. As Queen Hatshepsut was planning her temple, she had a vision of the god Amon-Ra. In the vision he told her to plant myrrh trees from Punt on the temple's terraces. Hatshepsut lost no time in organizing an expedition. When it returned, she was so pleased with the results that she had the story of the journey carved on the temple walls.

Instead of crossing the desert by caravan and building ships on the Red Sea, as Hannu had done, Hatshepsut's expedition sailed directly from the city of Coptos. Coptos lies on the banks of the Nile River, far from the Red Sea. This could mean that, by 1500 B.C., a canal of some sort connected the Nile with the Red Sea.

Oasis on the Red Sea

Led by a nobleman named Nehsi, the expedition set out with five large ships. Pictures on the temple walls show the ships being loaded in Coptos with every kind of Egyptian merchandise—fine cotton and linen cloth, cosmetics, and pottery. These would be unloaded in Punt in exchange for that country's priceless goods.

Remarkably, these five ships looked almost identical to Hannu's, built nine hundred years earlier. There are the same flat hulls and square sails, the same rows of standing oarsmen. The stern of one ship curves back upon itself in the graceful shape of a lotus flower and, for the first time in history, we can see a sounding pole being used to check the depth of the water.

A painting at Deir al-Bahri, Egypt, showing Egyptians transporting myrrh trees from the Land of Punt

Nehsi and his crew made their way down the Red Sea, very possibly without a map or a compass—and, it seems, without any difficulty. Pictures on the temple walls show them being lavishly welcomed by the king and queen of Punt.

The inscription goes on to tell us that the five ships returned to Egypt, heavily loaded "with marvels of the land of Punt, all goodly fragrant woods of God's land, heaps of myrrh resin, with fresh myrrh trees, ebony and pure ivory, gold of Emu, cinnamon wood, two kinds of incense, eye-cosmetic, apes, monkeys, dogs, skins of the southern panther, along with natives and their children. Never was brought the like of this for any king who has been since the beginning."

Queen Hatshepsut was so thrilled with Nehsi's success that she ordered a two-day holiday to celebrate the return of his ships. As she planted the sweet-smelling myrrh trees on the terraces of Amon-Ra's temple, it is written that she said joyfully, "I have made for him a Punt in his garden. It is large enough for him to walk about in."

This concludes the story of the ancient Egyptian explorers. They traveled the Nile, sailed the eastern Mediterranean, and ventured into the Red Sea to the fabled Land of Punt. But for the most part, Egyptians were a home-loving people who did not stray far from their native land. For true adventure-loving, seafaring explorers, we must now look across the Mediterranean to the island people of Crete.

Queen Hatshepsut's mortuary temple at Deir al-Bahri

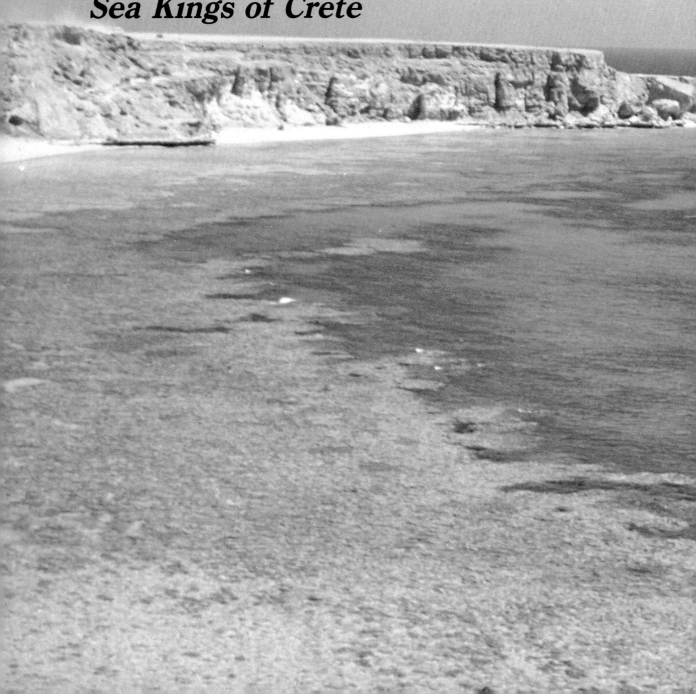

Chapter 3
Sea Kings of Crete

At the southern tip of the Aegean Sea, just at the point where it flows into the Mediterranean, lies the small island of Crete. Towering, snow-covered mountains rise from its center, gradually giving way to scrubby hillsides and then long, sandy beaches. Looking at Crete on a map, one would never guess that it was home to one of the ancient world's greatest civilizations—and to one of its greatest myths.

Legend has it that once, long ago, Crete was home to a fierce, terrifying monster called the Minotaur. Half man, half bull, the Minotaur was said to have an appetite for human flesh. The Minotaur was confined in a huge labyrinth. This was a maze of twisted corridors and winding passages, from which no one could escape. To satisfy the Minotaur's taste for human flesh, the Cretans offered it captives taken from neighboring islands.

No one knows exactly who or what the Minotaur really was. But we do know that there was a real labyrinth on Crete and that the kingdom of Crete demanded tribute from its Mediterranean neighbors.

Minotaur depicted in a fresco at Knossos, Crete

At Knossos, on the northern shore of Crete, archaeologists have uncovered the remains of an ancient city. And at the center of this city lie the ruins of a fabulous palace, whose long, winding hallways very much resemble a labyrinth. According to Greek legend, the palace at Knossos belonged to the powerful King Minos, who ruled Crete at the height of its power. Among the many things for which King Minos was famous were the elaborately staged bullfights he held during great national festivals.

Exactly what relationship the real King Minos had to the myth of the Minotaur will probably never be known. But from the remains at Knossos, we can tell that the Minoan period in Crete's history, from about 3000 B.C. to about 1400 B.C., was truly a golden one.

Imagine this. Four thousand years ago, the Cretans lived in houses with steam heating, running water, flush toilets, stoves, and even elevators. They were more modern than people living in the United States just two hundred years ago! The Cretans were not only skilled in technical things. Their pottery was known throughout the ancient world, and their work in inlaid bronze, gold, and ivory was eagerly bought by all who could afford it.

But first and foremost, the Cretans were a seafaring people. Surrounded by the sea, they could never resist its call. And since their small island had few natural resources, they had to rely on trade with other nations for the goods they needed. Then, too, once they realized the value of their own pottery and metalwork, they traveled far and wide to sell it to other peoples throughout the ancient world.

Above: Conical vessel in the Museum of Herakleion on the island of Crete

Below: Plan of the palace at Knossos

Unfortunately, we have very little firsthand knowledge of their explorations. The Minoans did keep records on stone tablets. To this day, however, we have not been able to decipher many of the tablets. So we must rely on what other people—the Egyptians and Greeks, mainly—have said about them. And we must look at the physical evidence, the Cretan objects that have been found in lands all around the Mediterranean.

From this evidence we know that, by 2200 B.C., Minoan merchant ships were protected by armed naval ships, making Crete the first naval power in history. With this protection, Cretan seamen sailed to almost every corner of the Mediterranean. They headed south to Egypt and east to Phoenicia to trade pottery for wheat and timber. They went north along the Adriatic Sea to buy amber for their ladies' jewelry. Far to the west were the Aeolian Islands, where they quarried

Painting on a Cretan sarcophagus, or stone coffin, showing an offering of sacrifices

stones for their temples and palaces. Sardinia provided copper, the Balearic Islands yielded bronze, and there is evidence that these daring sailors even made it as far west as Spain.

How did they do it? No remains of actual Minoan ships have ever been found, but pictures of them appear on many of their ancient coins and seals. From these pictures we can see that Cretan vessels looked nothing at all like the boats the Egyptians were using at about the same time. Instead of being long and flat, Cretan boats were small and tublike, with a deep keel and high stern. This made them better suited to open sea sailing than the Egyptian river boats. But like the Egyptian ships, Cretan vessels had a single square sail, which could be used only when the wind came up from behind. Otherwise, the ships were powered by rows of oarsmen, up to twenty per boat.

Painted clay vessel from the ancient Greek city of Mycenae, showing warriors leaving home

Dolphins depicted in a wall painting at the palace of Knossos in Crete

These sturdy little Cretan ships held no compasses to show direction, no sextants to measure distances, and no anchors. This meant that the sailors had to drag their boats up onto the beach every night—a strange practice for seagoing ships. Actually, though, the Cretans would have had to beach their ships every day anyway. There was no room in such small vessels for cooking, or even for storing much fresh food and water. And there certainly was no room for sailors to sleep! In fact, once the goods for trading had been taken aboard, there probably was not even much room for the sailors to sit and row. Going ashore each night must have been a relief for Minoan seamen!

Given the design of their ships and their lack of navigational aids, it is a wonder the Minoans made any sea voyages at all. In any sea but the Mediterranean,

The throne hall at Knossos

they probably would not have. In many ways the Mediterranean is more like a lake than a sea. It has mild, predictable winds; clear, starlit nights; and hardly any tides at all. Then, too, there are so many islands dotting the Mediterranean that one could sail from end to end without ever losing sight of land. The seafaring Minoans took advantage of all this to establish a maritime empire that lasted almost 1,500 years.

Then, suddenly, the Minoan civilization disappeared. No one knows exactly how or why, but by 1400 B.C. Crete's power had vanished. It is thought that invaders from Greece to the north destroyed the island kingdom around 1400 B.C. The magnificent palace at Knossos was destroyed, the navy was sunk, the people were killed. After 1,500 glorious years, the age of the Sea Kings of Crete had ended.

Chapter 4
Masters of the
Mediterranean

I f the Minoans were sea kings, then the people of ancient Phoenicia were sea lords. They were just coming into the height of their glory as the Minoans were losing theirs.

Home for the Phoenicians was a narrow, 100-mile (161-kilometer) strip of eastern Mediterranean coastline near present-day Israel and Lebanon. This is where they settled around 2750 B.C.

At about this same time, Egypt was abandoning its papyrus reed river boats for larger, stronger, wooden ships. Egypt did not have many trees, but Phoenicia did—miles and miles of magnificent cedar forests. So the people of Egypt began importing some of this timber to build their new ships. It was not long before the Phoenicians learned the art of shipbuilding themselves.

Ancient Phoenician sailors unloading treasures after a fruitful voyage

From there it was a short step to conquering the Mediterranean—and beyond. By 1475 B.C., Phoenician ships were making regular stops at Egyptian ports with their loads of timber. By 1300 B.C. they had made their way through the Red Sea to the east coast of Africa. In the opposite direction, they sailed along the coasts of Arabia and Persia all the way to India in search of ivory, gold, and spices. They transported wheat from Egypt, sheep and goats from Arabia, emeralds and embroidery from Syria. Whatever the ancient world had to trade, Phoenician merchant ships were willing to transport. And while they charged a high price for their services,

Servants cutting the highly valued cedar trees of Phoenicia

their clients did not mind. They knew the Phoenicians would go to almost any length to get the goods they wanted.

Phoenicia also had plenty of its own goods to trade. Timber from Phoenician cedar trees was always in great demand around the Mediterranean. But an even more desirable item was its exquisite purple dye. Very early in their history, Phoenicians had learned to make a beautiful red-purple dye from a tiny shellfish that lived just off the coast of the city of Tyre. This Tyrian dye-making process was kept strictly secret—and it made the dye-makers of Phoenicia rich.

By about 1200 B.C., Phoenicia was beginning to outgrow its narrow strip of coastline. Having mastered the markets of the eastern Mediterranean, it was time to look westward. So, following the old Cretan sailing routes, Phoenician mariners headed west across the Mediterranean. Past Cyprus, past Crete, past Sicily and Sardinia—Phoenician merchants sailed some 2,000 miles (3,219 kilometers) from their homeland. And as they traveled, they set up a chain of trading posts that stretched the full length of the Mediterranean.

Soon it seemed that even the Mediterranean Sea was too small to hold these adventurous Phoenician traders.

At the far west end of the Mediterranean Sea lies a narrow strait of water leading into the Atlantic Ocean. Today we know this as the Strait of Gibraltar. In ancient times it was called the Pillars of Hercules. Before the Phoenicians, no ancient mariners had dared to leave the friendly confines of the Mediterranean and sail beyond these pillars. But the Phoenicians dared. By 1100 B.C. they had established the port of Cades on the Atlantic Ocean. This port still exists as the city of Cadiz on the coast of present-day Spain.

Now it could truly be said that Phoenicians ruled the Mediterranean. By 800 B.C. their city of Carthage, located on the northern coast of Africa, was the largest and richest city in the western Mediterranean. No ships could enter that part of the sea without Carthaginian permission.

Phoenician boats did not look much like the Minoan vessels. Instead of being squat and tublike, they were long and narrow. This made them easier to navigate, and it made them faster. A Phoenician boat could travel about 100 miles (161 kilometers) a day. They still had the single sail, though, backed up by oarsmen who

rowed when the boats had to sail against the wind. But here again, the Phoenicians improved on Minoan ship design, for they had learned to cover their decks. That is, instead of a single row of oarsmen, Phoenician ships used double—or even triple—rows. Boats with double rows of oarsmen were called biremes. Ships with three banks of oars were known as triremes. With twice or triple the manpower, Phoenician ships could carry twice—or triple—the cargo.

Above: The Strait of Gibraltar
Below: A Phoenician bireme, a ship with two banks of oars

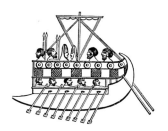

Beach along Turkey's Black Sea coast

Carrying cargo was what the Phoenician merchant ships were all about. By 600 B.C., Phoenicia was the center of a rich and far-flung empire. From the Atlantic Ocean to the Black Sea, from Arabia to Spain, from Italy to Persia, from Egypt to Lebanon, the Phoenicians plied their trade. Wherever the goods were, there the Phoenicians were. No danger seemed too threatening for their sailors.

In fact, the only thing that *would* threaten Phoenicia was the possibility that another country might try to compete with its trade. To prevent this, the Phoenicians developed a remarkable talent for keeping secrets. The design of their ships, the routes they traveled, the navigational aids they used—all were kept strictly secret from their neighbors.

This secretiveness was, of course, frustrating for the other countries that would have liked to move in on the Phoenician trade market. And it is almost equally frustrating for us today. Since the Phoenicians were careful not to keep records that might fall into the wrong hands, we have very few clues to tell us how they accomplished their amazing feats of seamanship.

There were some things that the Phoenicians simply would not talk about. And there were other things that they just would not *stop* talking about: Monstrous sea serpents that swallowed ships in a single gulp. Swirling whirlpools from which no sailor could escape. Foreign lands where the sun never shone—lands filled with raging giants, flying dragons, and six-headed monsters. To hear the Phoenicians talk, you would think the seas they sailed were all thick with mud and filled with rocks. No wonder the other ancients were hesitant to sail the Phoenician sea routes.

That is just what the Phoenicians wanted, of course—to frighten off anyone who had ideas about following them. Their tall tales worked for a while. But in the end, the Phoenicians were left with nothing but a reputation for being the biggest liars the world had ever known.

This, then, was the background for the adventurers described in Chapter One. Himilco and Hanno were both Phoenicians, and their daring trips beyond the Pillars of Hercules proved the courage and hardiness of Phoenician seamen. But the Phoenicians are famous for another trip, too. This one was even more daring and dangerous than those attempted by Hanno and Himilco.

Unfortunately, we do not know as much as we would like about this journey of exploration. Supposedly, it took place in about 600 B.C., but the only record we have was written almost two hundred years later. As the Greek historian Herodotus tells it, the Phoenicians were sailing under the orders of the Egyptian King Necho. Their orders were simple. King Necho wanted the Phoenicians to sail down the Red Sea into the Indian Ocean, and then all the way around Africa's east side and up its west coast.

It was the first time in history that such a voyage had been undertaken. In 600 B.C., no one knew how far Africa extended, or even if there were an ocean at its southern end. There were no accurate maps of the globe, no measurements of precise distances, no real knowledge of lands beyond the Mediterranean and Near East. No one but a fool would undertake such a hazardous, uncertain journey!

No one but a fool, or a Phoenician. Here is the story as Herodotus told it, some two hundred years later:

"As for Libya [an ancient name for Africa], we know it to be washed on all sides by the sea, except where it is attached to Asia. This discovery was first made by Necho, the Egyptian king, who sent forth Phoenician men in ships, ordering them to sail back between the Pillars of Hercules until they came to the Mediterranean Sea and thus to Egypt. The Phoenicians therefore setting forth from the Red Sea sailed in the Southern Ocean [the Indian Ocean]. When autumn came, they went ashore wherever they might happen to be, and having sown the land with corn, stayed until the grain was fit to cut. Having reaped it, they again set sail, and thus it came to pass that two whole years went by. It was not until the third year that they doubled the Pillars of

Egyptian King Necho employs Phoenician navigators to explore the coast of Africa

Hercules and made good their voyage home. And they told many things believable perhaps for others but unbelievable for me, namely that in sailing around Libya they had the sun upon their right hand. In this way was the extent of Libya first discovered."

So—were the Phoenicians telling the truth? Did they in fact take three years to sail some 13,000 miles (20,921 kilometers) around Africa? Or was this just another of their tall tales?

Herodotus got the story from the Egyptians. He was certainly more inclined to believe them than to believe the notoriously untruthful Phoenicians. If Herodotus had not thought there was at least some grain of truth to the tale, he would not have included it in his histories.

For a modern reader, the one detail that Herodotus found unbelievable is the very thing that tends to prove the story. That is the part about the sun being "upon their right hand" as the Phoenicians sailed around Africa.

Here is the explanation. In the Northern Hemisphere, where Herodotus and the rest of the peoples of the Mediterranean lived, the sun is always slightly to the south. But for people in the Southern Hemisphere, the sun appears to the north. When the Phoenicians sailed past the equator and south around the Cape of Good Hope (Africa's southern tip), the sun would have been on their right—to the north. Herodotus, who had never traveled south of the equator, would have known nothing about this. But from our vantage point in history, it makes perfect sense.

Still, the fact that it makes sense does not make the story true. We have no hard, physical evidence to prove Herodotus's tale. And until we find some, we will probably never know for sure whether or not the Phoenicians really sailed all the way around Africa over two thousand years ago.

But there is an interesting event later in history that supports the Phoenicians' claim. Around 120 B.C., a Greek merchant, Eudoxus of Cyzicus, set out on a trading voyage for Egypt's fabled Queen Cleopatra. Eudoxus had already become famous as the first person on record to sail directly from Egypt to India. He was not a man to refuse a challenge, and when Cleopatra

The Greek historian Herodotus

Queen Cleopatra of Egypt

asked him to make a second such voyage, he eagerly agreed.

History shows that Eudoxus made it safely across the sea from Egypt to India. On the way home, however, he was carried off course by strong winds. His ship was eventually driven ashore far down the east coast of Africa. When he landed, friendly natives showed him the wooden prow of a boat, with a horse carved on it. The prow looked remarkably like those of the merchant ships from the Phoenician port of Cades. And sure enough, the Africans assured Eudoxus that the prow was from the wrecked ship of men from the west.

A Phoenician galley, rowed by oarsmen inside the ship

As the story goes, "From this fact Eudoxus concluded that the circumnavigation of Libya [Africa] was possible. He went home ... and everywhere proclaiming his scheme and raising money, he built a great ship and also two tow-boats like those used by pirates. And he put music-girls on board and physicians and other artisans and finally set sail on the high sea. ..."

Unfortunately, Eudoxus never made it around Africa. His first boat was wrecked, and his plans for a second voyage were at first unsuccessful. But finally Eudoxus was ready to set sail once again. The story continues thus: "And again Eudoxus built a round ship and a long ship of fifty oars, his purpose being to keep to the open sea with his long ship and to explore the coast with the round ship. He put on board tools for farming, seeds, and carpenters, and again set out with the view to the same circumnavigation. His intention was, in case the voyage should be delayed, to spend the winter on an

Portuguese navigator Vasco da Gama, the first European to sail around the southern tip of Africa

island, to sow the seed, reap the harvest therefrom, and then finish the voyage which he had decided upon. . . ."

And that is the last we hear of Eudoxus. Did he in fact ever set sail? Were his ships wrecked by some storm at sea? Or was he washed ashore and killed by unfriendly natives? Perhaps his crew mutinied somewhere along the long voyage, or they were attacked by the Arab pirates that were a constant threat in those days. All we know is that neither Eudoxus nor any trace of his ships was ever seen again.

But the fact remains that, in 120 B.C., Eudoxus found the prow of a Phoenician boat on the far southeastern coast of Africa. This means that sometime before then, someone had once come close to sailing around the African continent. Given their daring and resourceful nature, it does not seem at all impossible that it was the sea lords from Phoenicia. Not until Vasco da Gama set sail in 1497 did any other explorer duplicate this feat.

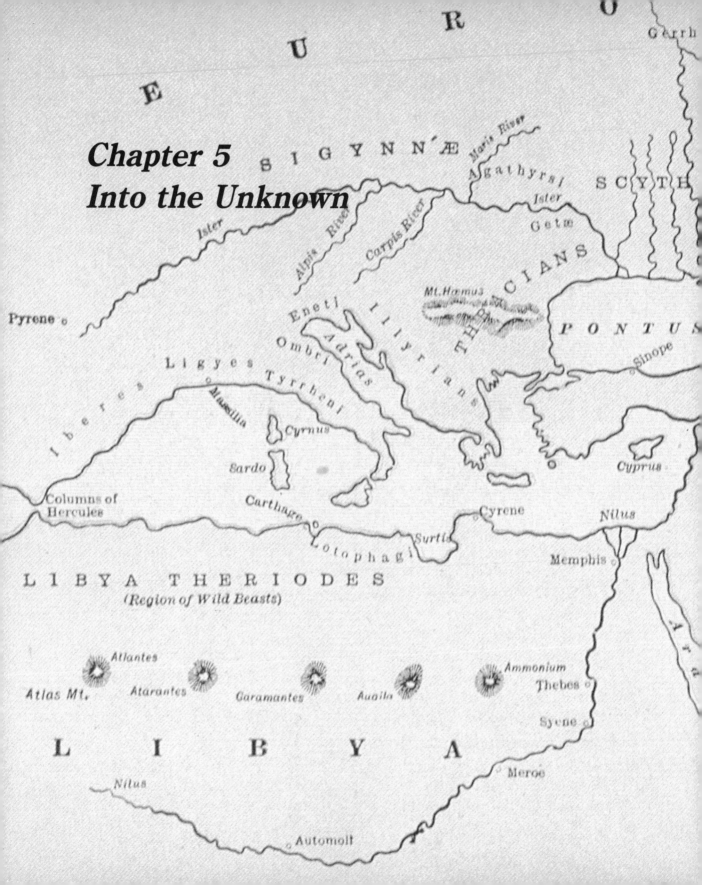

Chapter 5
Into the Unknown

EUROPE

SIGYNNÆ

Maris River

Agathyrsi

SCYTH

Garrh

Ister

Alpis River

Corpis River

Ister

Getæ

Mt. Hæmus

THRACIANS

PONTUS

Pyrene

Eneti

Adrias

Illyrians

Sinope

Ombri

Iberes

Ligyes

Tyrrheni

Massilia

Cyrnus

Cyprus

Sardo

Columns of
Hercules

Carthage

Cyrene

Nilus

Lotophagi

Surtis

Memphis

Arabia

LIBYA THERIODES
(Region of Wild Beasts)

Atlantes

Ammonium

Thebes

Atlas Mt.

Atarantes

Garamantes

Augila

Syene

L I B Y A

Nilus

Meroe

Automoli

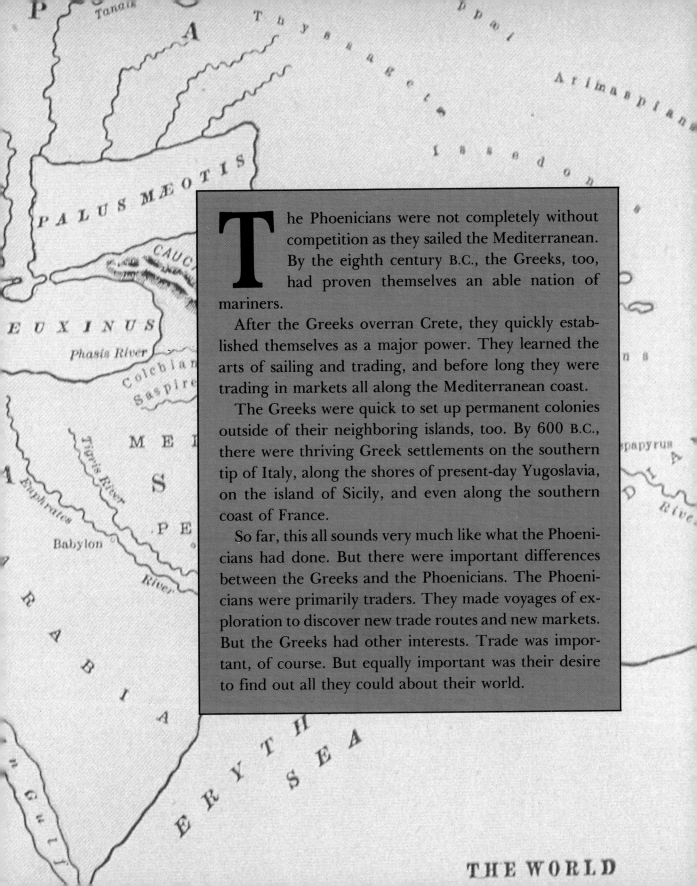

The Phoenicians were not completely without competition as they sailed the Mediterranean. By the eighth century B.C., the Greeks, too, had proven themselves an able nation of mariners.

After the Greeks overran Crete, they quickly established themselves as a major power. They learned the arts of sailing and trading, and before long they were trading in markets all along the Mediterranean coast.

The Greeks were quick to set up permanent colonies outside of their neighboring islands, too. By 600 B.C., there were thriving Greek settlements on the southern tip of Italy, along the shores of present-day Yugoslavia, on the island of Sicily, and even along the southern coast of France.

So far, this all sounds very much like what the Phoenicians had done. But there were important differences between the Greeks and the Phoenicians. The Phoenicians were primarily traders. They made voyages of exploration to discover new trade routes and new markets. But the Greeks had other interests. Trade was important, of course. But equally important was their desire to find out all they could about their world.

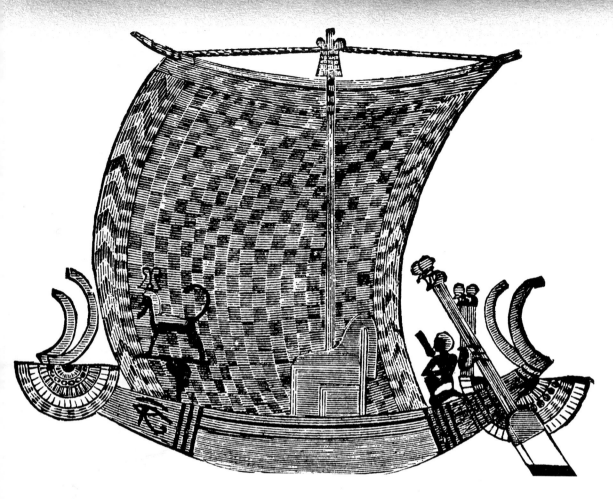

An Egyptian royal boat, from a sculptured tomb

The Greeks were not content with secondhand information about this world. First they studied the reports of earlier voyages by Phoenicians, Egyptians, and Minoans. Then they began to take voyages for no other reason than to explore and learn about distant lands.

Unlike the Phoenicians, the Greeks kept careful records of all they learned. In fact, it was a Greek who made the first map of the world. His name was Anaximander of Miletus, and he lived around 550 B.C. According to Anaximander, the world was flat and circular. The Mediterranean Sea formed the center of the world, and around it lay the lands of Asia, Europe, and Africa. Surrounding these landmasses, he believed, was a vast, unnamed ocean.

Anaximander's map has disappeared over the centuries. But scholars think it must have been very similar to a map drawn by the Greek historian Hecataeus, who lived some fifty years later. Hecataeus was probably the first person in Western civilization to undertake travels for purely scientific reasons. He visited as many lands as he could—Egypt and Persia as well as the regions around the Mediterranean—before he sat down to write his books and draw his maps. Even so, Hecataeus clearly had a limited view of the world. He, too, placed the Mediterranean Sea in the center of the world, with Europe, Libya, Arabia, and India surrounding it. Again, circling the whole thing, was a vast, vague, watery ocean.

Map of the world according to Hecataeus, a Greek historian of the fifth century B.C.

THE WORLD
according to
HECATÆUS
(500 B.C.)

The most famous Greek historian and geographer of them all, however, was Herodotus. Living from around 484 B.C. to 425 B.C., Herodotus is sometimes called the Father of History. He was an explorer and geographer who visited virtually every corner of the known world before writing a word. His travels took him from mainland Greece to the Aegean Islands and the Black Sea coast; through the Persian Empire and Arabia; into Egypt and Africa; and north through Italy into Europe. Although Herodotus did not discover new worlds, he did establish once and for all the limits and features of the lands that were already known.

Around the same time, a Greek scholar named Pythagoras was trying to convince people that the earth

Herodotus reading his history to an assembly of Greeks

Above: The Greek philosopher and mathematician Pythagoras giving a lesson
Below: Aristotle, ancient Greek philosopher and student of Plato

was round instead of flat. This was a new and strange idea for the time. As you can imagine, not everyone believed Pythagoras. One person who did was the philosopher and teacher Aristotle. And so did Aristotle's most famous pupil, the Greek ruler Alexander the Great.

Alexander the Great, who lived from 356 to 323 B.C., was without a doubt the greatest military leader of ancient times. From boyhood he had dreamed of conquering the world—and as a young man that is what he set out to do. His military campaigns took him through the deserts of Arabia and the plains of Persia; over the mountains of what are now Afghanistan and Turkey; and south into the Punjab region of India. For ten years and 10,000 miles (16,093 kilometers) Alexander's army marched through a vast, new, unexplored world.

Wounded king Poras stands before Alexander the Great after the Battle of Hydapses in 328 B.C.

Eventually, however, Alexander's exhausted soldiers mutinied and insisted on returning home. Weeping that there were no more lands for him to conquer, Alexander bowed to their demands. The army would return to Greece. But they would not all return by the same route. Determined to keep exploring, Alexander split his army in two. Half the group would march home, following the coastlines of the Indian Ocean and Persian Gulf to the familiar lands of Babylonia. The other half would sail home, in the hopes of finding a manageable sea route from the riches of India to the Mediterranean.

Alexander chose a man named Nearchus to captain the Greek fleet. With one hundred fifty ships and five thousand men under his command, Nearchus made his way through seas never before traveled by western sailors. It was an incredible journey. Battling storms and seasickness and huge schools of whales, suffering from hunger and thirst, cold and heat, the Greeks pressed on. When at last they reached the mouth of the Euphrates River on the Persian Gulf, the sailors were exhausted—and exhilarated. Not only had a vast new portion of the world been explored, but a new sea route to the East had been opened.

Above: Alexander the Great, king of Macedonia and conqueror of Greece and Persia
Below: Head of Alexander the Great

Right: Painting of the young Alexander the Great by Giovanni Battista Tiepolo
Below: Alexander dying

Within a year after Nearchus's sailors rejoined the Greek foot soldiers on the Euphrates, Alexander the Great was dead. He was only thirty-three years old. Shortly after that, his great empire began to fall apart.

But Alexander's deeds live on. Besides being a great general and explorer, he was also the first explorer to treat his travels in a scientific manner. Wherever he went, Alexander took with him distance measurers, naturalists, historians, and philosophers. Every step of his exploration was carefully recorded and studied, in an effort to further understand the world. Alexander the Great can truly be said to have begun a new era in geographic discovery.

Alexander was not the only great explorer of his time. While he was discovering new lands to the east, another Greek was exploring lands to the west and north. His name was Pytheas, from the Greek colony of Massilia.

In 330 B.C., Massilia (located on the site of today's French port of Marseilles) was a thriving center of trade. Its greatest rival was the Phoenician port of Carthage. As we know, the Carthaginians controlled the Pillars of Hercules, the western gateway to the Atlantic Ocean. Sailors from Massilia were continually frustrated in their attempts to sail past the Carthaginian guard.

Why did they want to get through the Pillars of Hercules? The people of this time lived in what we call the Bronze Age. Their strongest tools and weapons were made of bronze, a combination of copper and tin. Now, copper was plentiful in Cyprus and some of the Aegean Islands, but there was no tin in the eastern Mediterranean. For that, one had to travel through the Pillars of Hercules to the faraway Tin Islands. They were located somewhere in the north, in the land the Greeks called Europa. Otherwise, one had to pay fabulous sums to have tin and other valuable products carried overland through the plains of Europa.

By the time of Pytheas, the Greeks were tired of paying so much for tin and other rare European products. But sailing to the Tin Islands meant getting past the Phoenician fleet guarding the Pillars of Hercules.

That is just what Pytheas did. We are not sure exactly how he managed to sail past the Phoenicians, but sail he did—out into the Atlantic Ocean and up the coast of Spain. At first his ships—we do not know how many there were—followed the same path Himilco must have traveled over one hundred years earlier. But soon they were in unknown waters.

Goblets from the Mycenaean culture of ancient Greece

For sailors accustomed to the Mediterranean's calm waters and clear skies, the rough waves, strong currents, and thick fogs of the Atlantic must have come as a frightening surprise. The great ocean tides carried the Greek ships dangerously close to the rocky shores, then swung them out to sea again. When the wind was at their backs, sailing was relatively easy. But when the wind was against them, it took all the sailors' strength to man the oars and keep the ships on course.

Nevertheless, Pytheas and his men were determined to succeed. On they pushed, around the Bay of Biscay (west of present-day France) and across the English Channel. For the first time in recorded history, sailors were deliberately going out of sight of land. How frightening this must have been! Sailing without maps and compasses, early mariners needed to keep land in sight to know where they were and where they were going. For all Pytheas and his men knew, they could have been heading off the face of the earth.

When he reached the Channel Islands—Guernsey, Jersey, and Alderney—Pytheas thought he had finally reached his destination. But friendly natives of these ports said no. The precious tin was mined in another land farther north. Another day's sail—another 100 miles (161 kilometers)—and Pytheas was there. But he was in for yet another surprise. For the Tin Islands were not many islands at all. There was just one large island, with another large island off its west coast. Pytheas had discovered England and Ireland! And he had found the British tin mines of Cornwall.

Pytheas could have turned around and gone home then. He had found the tin mines. He had talked to the miners, made notes of their mining industry, and received assurances that they would be happy to trade di-

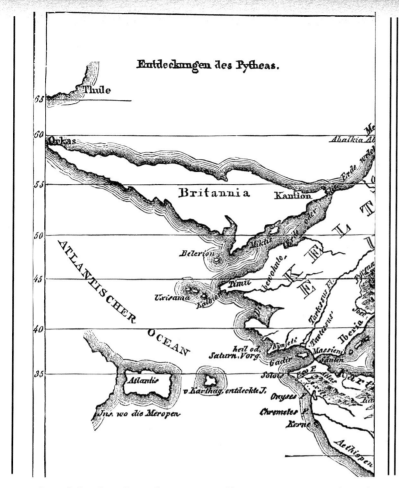

Detail of a map of the ancient world, showing the island of Thule as described by Pytheas

rectly with the Greeks. According to reports that have come to us over the centuries, this is how Pytheas described the people he met:

"The natives of Britain are ... unusually hospitable, and thanks to their meetings with foreign traders have grown gentle in their manner. They extract the tin from its bed by a cunning process. The bed is in rock, but contains earthy tunnels, into which they dig. And having smelted and refined it, they hammer it into knuckle-bone shape and take it to a nearby island named Ictis [St. Michael's Mount]. This island is surrounded by the sea at high water, but connected with the mainland by a tract of sand left bare at low water. Then do traders transport whole loads of tin on wagons southward."

Strictly speaking, Pytheas's mission was now over. But he was a scientist and an explorer as well as a merchant. As long as he had come this far, he wanted to learn more about these unknown lands of the north.

And so the boats sailed on. With frequent stops for fresh food and water—and to barter for warmer clothing!—they made their way up the coast of England to the far northern tip of Scotland. Through waves crashing as high as 90 feet (27 meters), through cold and rain and fog, the Greek ships pushed on. Their destination was an island the Britons called Thule. According to the Britons, Thule lay six days' sail to the north, in the middle of the Frozen Ocean. Here "there is neither sea nor air, but a mixture like sea-lung, in which earth and air are suspended; the sea-lung binds everything together."

Historians still do not know what to make of Thule. The Frozen Ocean and sea-lung sound like the Arctic Ocean, with its slushy packs of floating ice and dense fog. Thule could be Iceland, or it could be Norway, or it could be the Faeroe Islands. All we know is that Pytheas appears to have sailed until he could go no farther in the drifting pack ice.

Even then, Pytheas was not ready to return to Massilia. Instead, he continued his journey around Britain, making careful notes along the way about the people and their ways of life. From preserved fragments of his notes, we learn many details of the Britons' way of life:

"The people of Britain are . . . sprung from the soil and are very primitive . . . their houses are poor, being made of logs, mud, and straw. . . . They are simple in their habits and far removed from the cunning of modern man. . . . Their diet is simple, as they feed on corn and wild berries and roots. . . . They must thresh their corn in covered barns, because of the continual rain. . . . The island is thickly populated, and has an extremely chilly climate, as one would expect in sub-Arctic regions. . . . It has many kings, who live for the most part in a state of mutual peace."

Pytheas also mentioned a beverage the natives made from fermented barley. He called this drink "curmi." Today we realize that what he discovered was—beer!

Some historians believe that Pytheas then headed east into the North Sea toward the European mainland. He may have made it as far as Germany's Elbe River, in search of the prized amber that he knew was found in the area. According to a questionable report, he landed on the small island of Helgoland and saw raw amber washed up along the shore by the spring tides.

By now Pytheas was ready to come home. Some six years after he set out from Massilia, Pytheas sailed triumphantly back into home port. He and his men had sailed some 7,000 miles (11,265 kilometers) through unknown waters. When the wind was at their backs, the sailing had been relatively easy. But when the wind was against them, the sailors had had no choice but to row their way through the high seas of the Atlantic. Rowing their 150-foot (46-meter) boats—longer than those that Columbus sailed across the Atlantic some 1,800 years later!—had been no easy matter.

Once back home in Massilia, Pytheas sat down to write up the notes he had so carefully kept throughout his journey. These notes eventually made their way into two books, *The Ocean* and *The Periplus*. Unfortunately, both have been lost. All we have left are the comments written by scholars who read the books or who heard about them from other scholars.

What did Pytheas write about? As a scientist, he took careful note of the tides in the Atlantic. He was the first to suggest that they were caused by the moon—an observation in which he was 2,000 years ahead of his time. As an astronomer, he added greatly to the science of navigation. By figuring out the height of the sun by the length of the shadow it casts, he was able, for the first time in recorded history, to determine the latitudes of the places he visited. This made him the first person to apply astronomy to geography to locate a place on the earth. This became the basis of accurate mapmaking. As an anthropologist, he was the first to scientifically record the habits and customs of the peoples he visited.

Unfortunately, no one much appreciated Pytheas in his own time. In fact, many people called him a liar. They did not believe what he said about the size and strength of ocean currents. Why should they, when all they knew were the calm waters of the Mediterranean? No one believed that there was just one large Tin Island—why, they had been called the Tin *Islands* for as long as anyone could remember. Nor did people believe tales of a frozen, slushy sea—or of the land of Thule, which could support human life!

As the years went by, fewer and fewer people believed Pytheas's claims. Here is what the historian Strabo wrote, some three hundred years after Pytheas's journey:

"True, Pytheas of Massilia claims that the farthest country north of the British islands is Thule. . . . I think, for my part, that the northern boundaries of the habitable earth are much farther south. Modern writers tell us of nothing beyond Ireland, which lies just north of Britain, where people entirely savage live miserably because of the intense cold. Here, in my opinion, is where the bounds of the habitable earth should be fixed."

Today, of course, we know that much of what Pytheas said about Britain and the Atlantic and Arctic oceans is completely accurate. Iceland, Greenland, Scandinavia—all lie north of Ireland, and all are certainly habitable. It is true that Pytheas made some mistakes, especially when calculating distances. For example, he estimated that Britain was more than twice as big as it really is. But considering the tools he had to work with, Pytheas's achievements are nothing less than amazing. As an explorer, navigator, geographer, and observer of mankind, Pytheas remains one of the greatest explorers of all time.

Norwegian fjords. Pytheas may have seen similar sights on his great voyage.

69

Chapter 6
Chang Ch'ien:
The Great Traveler

All of the ancient explorers discussed so far have all lived in the Middle East or along the Mediterranean Sea. But one of the greatest explorers of the ancient world lived in China. His name was Chang Ch'ien. The story of how he opened up China's western frontier is as exciting today as when it happened two thousand years ago.

Chang Ch'ien's adventure began in 138 B.C., some two hundred years after the time of Pytheas. But unlike Pytheas, Chang Ch'ien was not a seafaring man. Instead of battling open seas and unknown coastlines, he faced the high mountains and wide plains of central Asia. Like Meriwether Lewis and William Clark of the American West, Chang Ch'ien was the pioneer of a long, dangerous, and historically important overland trail.

One reason that Chang Ch'ien's adventure is so exciting to us today is that it was so well recorded. The Chinese historian Ssŭ-ma Ch'ien (no relation to Chang Ch'ien) wrote the story two thousand years ago. Ssŭ-ma Ch'ien is sometimes called the Herodotus of China. Just as Herodotus set the pattern for writing history in Greece, so did Ssŭ-ma Ch'ien set the standard for writing history in China.

A traveler, scholar, and court astrologer, Ssŭ-ma Ch'ien prided himself on faithfully setting down the facts just as they happened. According to Ssŭ-ma Ch'ien, historians have the right to organize facts to make them readable and interesting—but never to change or add to those facts. His book, the *Shih-chi, Memoirs of an Historian,* was completed about 100 B.C. and has survived to the present. It is from this book that we have learned about Chang Ch'ien's explorations.

At the time of our story, Chang Ch'ien was an officer in the household of Wu-ti, emperor of China. Like Alexander the Great, the eighteen-year-old Wu-ti had become ruler of a powerful kingdom while he was still a boy. Wu-ti, though young, was shrewd enough to surround himself with loyal and able men. General Chang Ch'ien was one of these men.

Chang Ch'ien came from the mountain province of Shensi, where men were known for their strength and daring. It is no surprise that Emperor Wu-ti thought highly of him. According to Ssŭ-ma Ch'ien's description, Chang Ch'ien was an officer "of strong build, generous and trustful, and popular with the foreign tribes in the south and west."

Emperor Wu-ti had need of a strong and daring officer to serve him in a daring plan. For years, Wu-ti's kingdom had been under attack by fierce northern

漢
張
騫

The great explorer and adventurer
Chang Ch'ien

tribesmen known as the Hsiung-nu, or Huns. The time had come to put a stop to these attacks. Wu-ti's plan was to send a mission to another tribe, the Yüeh-chih, enlisting their help in defeating the Huns. The only problem was that nobody knew exactly where these Yüeh-chih lived. They had been driven out of their own homeland years before by the same Huns who were now bothering Wu-ti and his people. According to rumors, the Yüeh-chih had fled far to the north. Anyone trying to find them would have to travel miles through the trackless Gobi Desert. On the way, they would have to pass straight through the land of the fierce Huns.

China's Gobi Desert

It was to lead such a mission that Wu-ti chose Chang Ch'ien. Though the wise men of the court shook their heads at such an impossible task, Chang Ch'ien paid no attention. On a clear May morning, Chang Ch'ien set out to find the Yüeh-chih.

To really understand Chang Ch'ien's mission, one has to understand something about China and its history. Most of China is located on the great central plain of Asia. To the north of this plain lies the vast Gobi Desert and bleak, mountainous steppes. To the east is the Pacific Ocean; to the south, the South China Sea and the tropics of Southeast Asia; to the west, the high reaches of the Himalayan mountain range. Since history began, China has been cut off from the rest of the world by

these natural barriers. For centuries its civilization developed in isolation.

The ancient Chinese knew that other peoples existed, but they did not really care. Their civilization along the Hwang Ho, or Yellow River, was nearly as old as those along the Nile and the Euphrates. In their mind, they were the chosen people of heaven, and their emperor was the Son of Heaven. Just as the Egyptians and Greeks thought the Mediterranean was the center of the earth, so the Chinese believed their land to be the center of the earth. Anyone living outside this Middle Kingdom was dismissed as a barbarian. While at first the word "barbarian" meant "non-Chinese," it eventually came to have the scornful meaning with which we associate it today.

Huge sand dunes in the Gobi Desert along the road near Tunhuang

秦始皇

Chinese emperor Shih Huang-ti, who begun building the Great Wall as a protection against the Huns

For centuries, the Middle Kingdom had been subject to attack by its fierce Hun neighbors to the north. This situation improved after around 220 B.C., when Emperor Shih Huang-ti began building his protective Great Wall across the kingdom's northern boundaries. This wall, which eventually stretched 1,500 miles (2,414 kilometers) across northern China, still stands today. In fact, it is the only man-made structure on earth that is visible from the moon! But while the Great Wall slowed down the Hun warriors, it could not completely stop them. With as many as a quarter of a million archers on horseback under his command, the Hun chieftain con-

An 1835 drawing of the Great Wall

tinued to raid the more civilized people of the Middle Kingdom. Looting, burning, and killing, the Huns made life miserable for the Chinese.

By 138 B.C., the people of the Middle Kingdom had had enough. They had tried fighting back when the Huns attacked. They had tried bribing them, offering jewels, gold, silks—even their most beautiful women. They had even tried ignoring the Hun raids, in the feeble hope that their attackers would get tired of all the fighting and go home. But nothing worked. By Wu-ti's time, what should have been a prosperous kingdom was beginning to come apart at the seams.

So the Emperor Wu-ti did the only thing left to do. He decided to defeat the Huns once and for all in a full-fledged war. This is where the story of Chang Ch'ien begins. Wu-ti knew from bitter experience that, to win a war against the Huns, he needed allies to help him fight. And what better allies than the Yüeh-chih? Not only had the Huns driven them from their homeland, but they had brutally murdered many of their people. They had even made a drinking cup out of the skull of the Yüeh-chih's king! Surely these people would want to avenge themselves and their slain comrades by joining the Chinese in battle against the Huns.

Chang Ch'ien prepared for his journey carefully. Along with his personal servant, Kan Fu (who came from the north and spoke the Huns' language), he took along one hundred of the emperor's finest soldiers. He also took along a camel caravan loaded with the finest prizes of the Chinese empire. These costly items—silks, porcelains, and jewels—were gifts for the new king of the Yüeh-chih. Such valuable gifts would surely persuade him to help the Chinese in their war against the Huns.

At last Chang Ch'ien and his party set out in search of the Yüeh-chih. In the beginning, it looked as if the wise men of the court would be right. No sooner had the caravan passed beyond the Great Wall than it was attacked by a party of raiding Huns. Many of the Chinese were killed. The rest, including Chang Ch'ien and Kan Fu, were promptly taken prisoner by the Huns' khan, or leader, Lou Shang.

For ten long years Chang Ch'ien remained a captive. In spite of himself, the khan took a liking to his Chinese prisoner. As time went on, he allowed his captive more and more freedom. He even let Chang Ch'ien marry a

Hun princess, by whom Chang had a son. But Chang Ch'ien never forgot that he was on a mission for his emperor.

All the time he was held prisoner, he took careful notes of the Huns' customs, habits, and methods of warfare. If he ever escaped, the information would be invaluable to the Chinese armies.

One day Chang Ch'ien did escape. History does not tell us exactly how he managed this. We only know what Ssŭ-ma Ch'ien wrote: "When in the course of time Chang Ch'ien was permitted greater freedom, he watched his opportunity and succeeded in making his escape."

What dangers and hardships Chang Ch'ien faced after his escape, we do not know. All Ssŭ-ma Ch'ien tells us is that Chang Ch'ien, with his wife and child and a few soldiers, "marched several tens of days to the west." But we can imagine what the trek must have been like. Before the small band lay a vast, trackless desert; behind them were the vicious Huns.

Chang had learned from his Hun captives that the Yüeh-chih had moved west, not north. With no more directions than this, he led his party onward. For weeks they plodded through the raging sandstorms of the Gobi Desert. Blistered by the sun by day and frozen by bitter winds at night, the party kept heading westward for over 2,500 miles (4,023 kilometers). Finally they reached the Tien Shan Mountains, home to the friendly Ta-yuan people.

The Ta-yuan were impressed by Chang Ch'ien's story and eager to help the powerful Chinese empire. They offered both directions and escorts to the new homeland of the Yüeh-chih, which lay another 800 miles (1,287 kilometers) to the southwest.

Finally, in that part of Asia known as Bactria (near present-day Afghanistan), Chang Ch'ien found the Yüeh-chih. But to his disappointment, the Yüeh-chih were not interested in helping the Chinese fight the Huns. Things had gone well for them since they had been driven out of their old homeland. As Ssŭ-ma Ch'ien wrote:

"Since that time they had conquered Ta-hsia [Bactria] and occupied the country. It was a rich and fertile land, seldom harassed by robbers, and the people decided to enjoy this life of peace. Moreover, since they considered themselves too far away from China, they no longer wanted to avenge themselves on the Huns. After having made his way through so many tribes to find Bactria, Chang Ch'ien was unable to persuade the Yüeh-chih to move against their former enemy."

Magicians of ancient Persia

Despite this disappointment, Chang Ch'ien put his time with the Yüeh-chih to good use. From their king, he learned of a rich country to the south, Shon-ti (which we know as India), and another to the southwest, Parthia (Persia). And he learned of an even richer and more powerful country still farther to the west. The Yüeh-chih called it Ta-tsin, but to the western world it was the Roman Empire. Chang Ch'ien pondered this information carefully. Perhaps China was not the only civilized nation in the world. Knowing this could be important for Chang Ch'ien's emperor and for the Chinese empire.

From the Yüeh-chih, Chang Ch'ien heard news of the powerful Roman Empire, which was conquering faraway lands. This painting shows a Roman town at the foot of the Alps.

After a year, Chang Ch'ien bid the Yüeh-chih farewell. He left their kingdom with an abundance of new information—and with an invitation for the Chinese to start trading with the Yüeh-chih. Chang Ch'ien knew his emperor would welcome such an invitation. He loaded his pack train with an assortment of goods never before seen in China—spices and seeds, walnuts and grapevine cuttings. Best of all, the Yüeh-chih king gave Chang several beautiful horses as a gift to Emperor Wu-ti.

Unfortunately, these gifts were never to reach Wu-ti. Hoping both to avoid the Huns and to explore new lands on his way home, Chang Ch'ien chose a new route by which to return to China. Instead of going north, he took a southern route across the Tarim Basin (north of present-day Tibet) to the eastern end of the Takla Makan Desert. From there his route led him past the great salt lake of Lop Nor and into the foothills of the Nan Shan Mountains. And then, almost within sight of home, his luck ran out. Once again Chang Ch'ien met up with his old enemies, the Huns!

For the second time, Chang Ch'ien was thrown into prison. But this time he managed to escape after only a year. In 126 B.C., twelve long years after he set out on his mission, Chang Ch'ien returned to China, accompanied by his wife, his son, and the faithful Kan Fu.

Astonished to see his old officer, Wu-ti was very impressed when Chang Ch'ien told of his twelve-year adventure. It was true that Chang Ch'ien had failed in his original mission, to convince the Yüeh-chih to fight with the Chinese against the Huns. But he had succeeded in learning many of the Huns' battle secrets. Wu-ti's warlords lost no time in putting this information to good use. Now, for the first time in history, the Chinese began winning their war against the Huns.

There is no doubt that the information Chang Ch'ien brought back about the Huns was valuable to the Chinese. But equally valuable was the other information he had gathered during the course of his travels. He had explored vast and previously unknown territories of Asia. He had established friendly relations with civilized peoples along the route. And he had learned of other civilized peoples in Persia, India, and Rome.

Chang Ch'ien's reports opened up a whole new world for the Chinese. Of Parthia he wrote, "They make coins of silver; the coins resemble their king's face. Upon the death of a king the coins are changed for others on which the new king's face is represented. They paint rows of characters running sideways on stiff leather to serve them as records." (This was surprising to the Chinese, who write from top to bottom.)

Of Ferghana, an oasis valley in central Asia famous for its thoroughbred horses, Chang Ch'ien reported: "The people have wine made of grapes and many good horses. The horses sweat blood and come from the stock of heavenly horses." Horses were not native to China, and Wu-ti lost no time in securing some of these heavenly mounts to use in his war against the Huns.

Perhaps most importantly, Chang Ch'ien had learned that the people of the West were interested in goods produced in China—and that Westerners had riches for which China could trade in return.

Wu-ti heaped many honors upon Chang Ch'ien for his remarkable discoveries. He appointed him first the lord of Po-wang and later, the Great Traveler, or head of the office of foreign affairs. Exploring parties were sent out to the friendly tribes that Chang Ch'ien had met on his journey. Wars were fought, as well, to overcome the not-so-friendly tribes.

A great trade route grew up in central Asia after Chang Ch'ien pioneered the way.

Thanks to Chang's explorations, China eventually extended its rule clear across the Tarim Basin. New trade routes were established, fortified by a chain of military posts to protect travelers.

Chang Ch'ien himself led another expedition to the West eleven years later. His reports from this expedition, along with those of his earlier trek, resulted in the opening of China's famous silk route. For hundreds of years thereafter, camel trains would travel this 2,000-mile (3,219-kilometer) trade route. Loaded with China's precious silks, porcelains, and spices, some caravans plodded west across the vast Gobi Desert and the icy Pamir Plateau to Parthia. Others headed south across Tibet to India. Greek, Arab, and Roman traders then carried the goods thousands of miles on to the markets of the Mediterranean and the European interior.

Before Chang Ch'ien, there had been virtually no contact between China and the West. But because of this intrepid explorer's determination and courage, his country opened its doors. Through both trade and military conquest, China gradually extended its influence throughout all of Asia—and even into Europe and the Mediterranean region.

Chang Ch'ien's explorations helped change the face of the ancient world. They also affected commerce for centuries to come. As the historian Ssŭ-ma Ch'ien wrote: "Since Chang Ch'ien had been the pioneer in this [trade between China and the West], envoys proceeding to the West after him always referred to the Marquis of Po-wang as an introduction in foreign countries, the mention of his name being regarded as a guaranty of good faith."

A tiny Chinese pottery sculpture from Hunan province, showing traders along the silk route

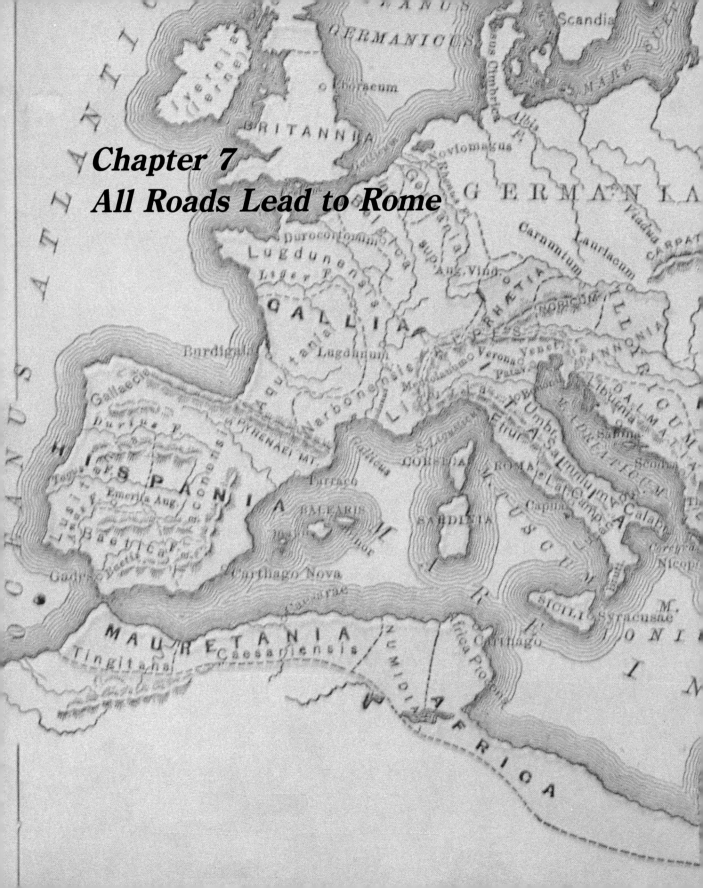

Chapter 7
All Roads Lead to Rome

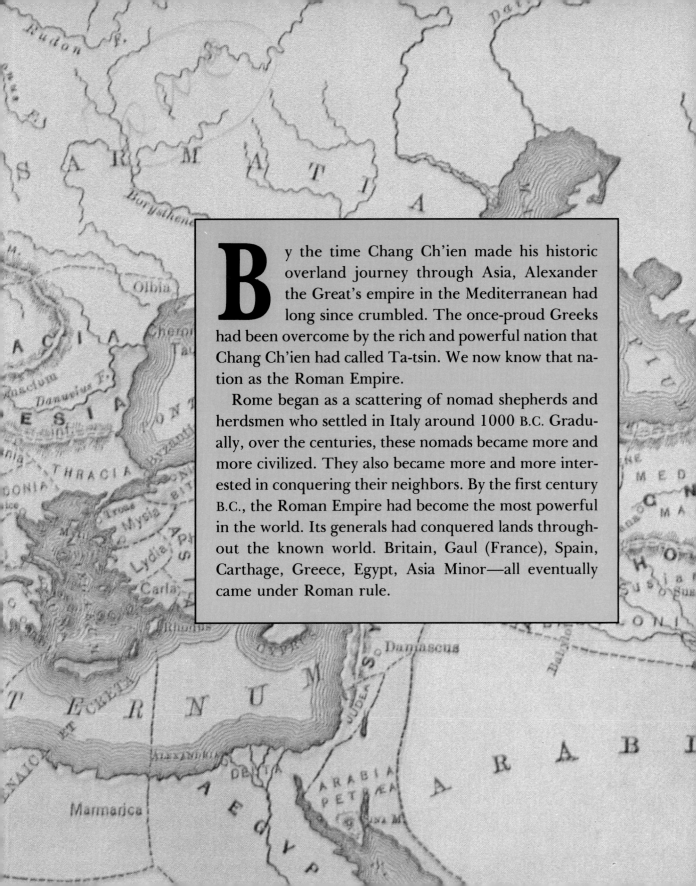

By the time Chang Ch'ien made his historic overland journey through Asia, Alexander the Great's empire in the Mediterranean had long since crumbled. The once-proud Greeks had been overcome by the rich and powerful nation that Chang Ch'ien had called Ta-tsin. We now know that nation as the Roman Empire.

Rome began as a scattering of nomad shepherds and herdsmen who settled in Italy around 1000 B.C. Gradually, over the centuries, these nomads became more and more civilized. They also became more and more interested in conquering their neighbors. By the first century B.C., the Roman Empire had become the most powerful in the world. Its generals had conquered lands throughout the known world. Britain, Gaul (France), Spain, Carthage, Greece, Egypt, Asia Minor—all eventually came under Roman rule.

As Rome's power grew, so did its taste for the spoils of war. Over the years, Romans had become used to the luxuries that came from their newly conquered lands. Pearls and precious stones from India, ebony and ivory from Africa, spices and perfumes from Arabia—all were eagerly sought by the high-born men and women of imperial Rome.

The Romans themselves did not care much for sea voyages. They preferred to leave the transporting of these precious goods to others. Even after Rome had conquered Greece, Greek sailors continued to roam the seas. But now, instead of seeking out knowledge of the world and its boundaries, Greek mariners were seeking out oriental luxuries for their Roman masters.

In those days, the world's greatest center of trade and

The prow of an ancient Roman galley

commerce was Alexandria. This Egyptian port was located at the mouth of the Nile River, at the eastern edge of the Mediterranean. It was an easy sail from Alexandria across the Mediterranean and up the coast of Italy to Rome.

Merchants sailing to the East from Alexandria, however, did not have such an easy time of it. First they traveled on river boats up the Nile to the city of Coptos. Next, camel caravans took them across the desert to the Red Sea ports of Myos Hormos and Berenice. There, oceangoing vessels were outfitted for the long journey down the Red Sea and out into the Erythraean Sea (today's Arabian Sea and Indian Ocean). From there, they followed ports that lay like stepping-stones along the coasts of Africa, Arabia, Persia, and India.

Transporting merchandise along the silk route

Thus Rome's trade with the East flourished. By the first century A.D., the Roman historian Strabo wrote, "as many as a hundred and twenty vessels were sailing from Myos Hormos to India in a single year."

The voyagers, however, met with serious problems along the way. The coast-hugging sea voyage along Arabia and Persia was long and difficult—and expensive. If pirates did not rob the merchant ships, tax collectors at Arabian and Persian ports did. There had to be a better way—and there was. It was discovered by a Greek merchant named Hippalus early in the first century A.D. Here is what happened.

Ever since the time of Alexander the Great, the Greeks had known about the winds we now call monsoons. These monsoon winds blow regularly across the

Roman mariners engaged in a battle at sea

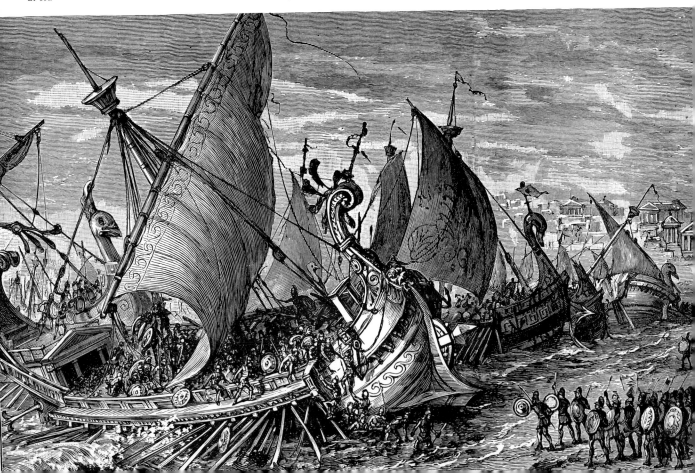

Sailing the coastal waters could be dangerous

Indian Ocean and the Bay of Bengal. In the winter, they blow from east to west, from India to Africa. In the summer, they reverse themselves. Then they blow from west to east, from Africa to India, and even beyond to Burma and Thailand.

But though the Greeks had known about these winds for three hundred years, no one had put them to practical use. No one until Hippalus, that is. One fine summer day, this remarkable man set out from the mouth of the Red Sea straight across the open ocean. According to Hippalus's calculations, he should not have to hug the coastlines of Arabia and Persia. Nor, he felt, should he have to watch out for pirates in hidden coves or pay tribute to port authorities. Driven by the summer monsoon, he would breeze straight across the sea to India.

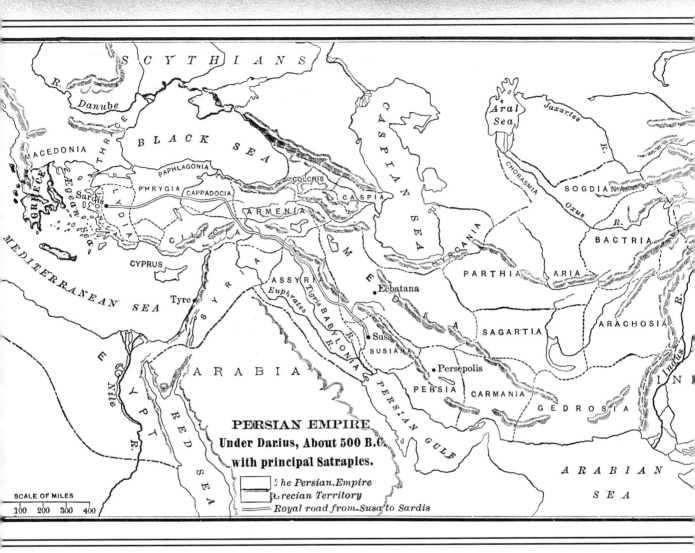

Map of the Persian empire

And so he did. After sailing across some 1,500 miles (2,414 kilometers) of open water, Hippalus put in to port near the mouth of the Indus River in northern India. His historic journey a success, Hippalus calmly completed his trading and sailed home again when the monsoons reversed themselves the following November.

Hippalus's experiment opened up a whole new era in ancient trading. It also made this mild-mannered Greek merchant famous. His name was given to the monsoon blowing from west to east, to a cape on the African coast, and to part of the Arabian Sea!

As it turned out, however, Hippalus had taken just the first step in sailing to India. His monsoon took ships to northern Indian ports, but the most precious stones and spices were found in the south of India. In about A.D. 50, another Greek trader decided to try to reach those southern markets. He simply had his sailors steer the ship's rudder hard to the right all the way across the ocean. This kept the Greek ship on a southeasterly course. Sure enough, in forty days the ship came ashore near the southern town of Muziris, the greatest of all the Indian ports.

A Greek sailing ship known as a trireme, having three banks of oarsmen

About the same time, a tax collector named Annius Plocamus was sailing around Arabia. Suddenly, his ship was caught in an unexpected and previously unknown monsoon. The next thing Annius knew, he had been blown all the way to the south of India, to the island we now know as Sri Lanka. Once they understood this new monsoon, traders began sailing clear around India and into the Bay of Bengal.

Not all Greek traders were interested in crossing the ocean to India. While some merchants sailed east out of the Red Sea, others headed south. Their explorations took them some 1,500 miles (2,414 kilometers) down the east African coast, as far as present-day Tanzania. Here, in the great ancient marketplace of Rhapta, they traded for the ivory and tortoise shell so prized by Romans. And they put to rest forever the notion that people could not survive in the tropical lands south of the equator. The people of Rhapta even claimed that lands much farther south were inhabited. However, since these inhabitants were said to be cannibals, the Greek traders decided to take the Rhaptans' word for it instead of going off to see for themselves!

By now, Greek merchants had become such experienced travelers that guidebooks were being written for them. One such guidebook was the Periplus of the Erythraean Sea, written around A.D. 60 by an unnamed Greek trader.

This book guided the reader down the coast of Africa as far as Rhapta, and across the Indian Ocean and down the coast of India to Sri Lanka. The author described sailing routes and harbors. He even provided a handy list of trading centers, along with the merchandise that could be found in each. About one particularly treacherous Indian harbor, the guidebook said:

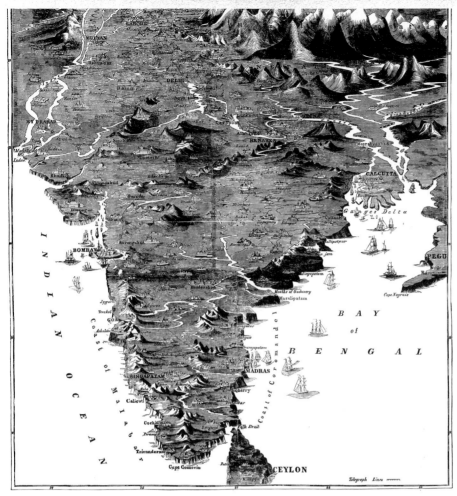

Map of India, showing the Indian Ocean and the Bay of Bengal

"The putting in and putting out of ships are dangerous for those sailing into the mart for the first time. For when there is a pull of water at the flood-tide, there is no withstanding it, nor do the anchors hold against it. For this reason, even big ships, caught by the force of it and turned broadside through the swiftness of the flow, run aground and break up, while smaller boats are even overturned."

The guide goes on, however, to reassure sailors that they need not be unduly alarmed. The Indian king who ruled this port had thoughtfully provided a towboat service for traders needing assistance in bringing their ships into port!

Ladies of ancient Rome

The next great step for the Greek traders was to cross the Bay of Bengal to the fabled eastern lands of Burma, Malaysia, and even China. Oddly enough, the ladies of Rome had a great deal to do with these advances.

The reason was simple. Of all the luxuries of the ancient world, the one in greatest demand was silk. Fine, shimmering, brilliantly colored—silk was the cloth of choice when the Roman noblewoman wanted to look her best. And silk was a most expensive luxury indeed. It was produced, thread by thread, by the tiny silkworm in faraway China. The silkworm's task was long and laborious, but getting the finished cloth from China to the western markets was even worse.

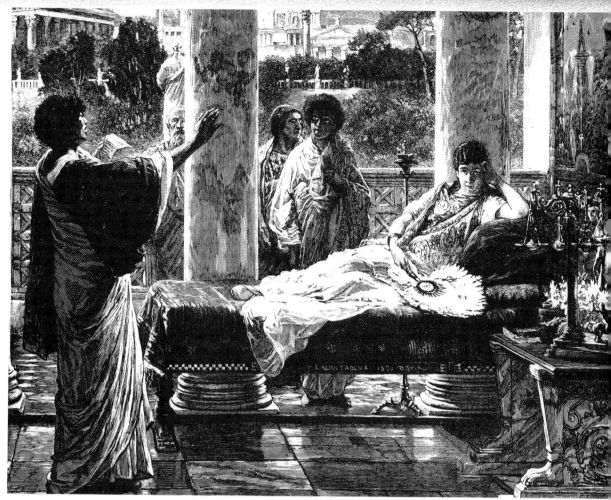

Gold, silk, marble, jewels, and other precious goods surrounded the Roman noblewoman.

Most of the time the silk came to Rome via India, and the road from China to India was long and tortuous. Silk crossed high mountains and wide desert plains; it traveled by camel caravan and river barge and ocean-going long ship. And every time it changed hands or crossed borders, its price went up. By the time the silk reached Rome, it was one of the most expensive luxuries known. Huge amounts of Roman gold were being spent on silk. At one point, Roman rulers worried that this might drain the nation's gold reserves!

Naturally, Western traders would have liked a more direct route to the land of the silkworm. It was another Greek merchant who found the way.

His name was Alexander, and he lived around A.D. 100. It occurred to Alexander that what had worked for Hippalus in the Erythraean Sea might work for him in the Bay of Bengal. And he was right. There were monsoons in this large bay to the east of India. They were not as strong or as regular as the monsoons to the west, but they got Alexander where he wanted to go.

However, Alexander was not satisfied with just sailing across the Bay of Bengal. He wanted to reach China—or, as the Romans named it, Sinae (meaning Silk Land). Onward he sailed, past Burma, through Malaysia, beyond Thailand, until at last, after three long years at sea, he reached the land of the silkworm, near present-day Vietnam.

Other adventurers followed. For the first time in history, Mediterranean merchants came in direct contact with Chinese merchants. The people of Ta-tsin, described to Chang Ch'ien some four hundred years earlier, had finally made their way to the Middle Kingdom.

It was important to Rome to establish friendly relations with its new trading partner. In A.D. 166, the Roman emperor Marcus Aurelius sent an embassy (a group of diplomats) to the Chinese emperor Huan-ti. With them Marcus sent gifts from the Roman people—gifts which the Chinese emperor was pleased to accept as "tribute"!

Thus the boundaries of the known world continued to expand. Old maps were no longer of any use, and new ones had to be drawn up. The most famous of these maps was created by a Greek geographer named Claudius Ptolemy around A.D. 140.

Ptolemy was an astronomer as well as a geographer. When he set out to "reform the map of the world," he did not merely want to draw pictures of countries and

oceans. He also hoped to establish a system for locating places on his map. He did this by drawing a network of east-west and north-south lines on his map. Thus Ptolemy created what we know today as the lines of latitude and longitude.

Ptolemy's map was much more complete than earlier maps had been. No longer was the Mediterranean Sea the center of the world. On it we see Europe, northern Africa, Arabia, Asia (which he called Scythia), India, China—even Pytheas's island of Thule.

But Ptolemy made some serious mistakes with his map. First, he made the world too small. He figured it to be about 18,000 miles (28,967 kilometers) in circumference. This was some 7,000 miles (11,265 kilometers) smaller than it really is.

Romans engaged in one of their many battles of conquest

Second, Ptolemy made his countries too large, so that they practically filled up the whole map. But we cannot really blame Ptolemy for this. When he drew his map, distances were measured mainly by days at sea or weeks on the caravan road. It was hard to draw an accurate map with measurements like these!

Another problem was that Ptolemy simply did not know what lay beyond the lands and oceans on his map. No one had ever been east of China or west of the Atlantic Ocean in those days. Ptolemy also drew the coast of Africa so that it turned eastward to connect with China. Either he did not know of, or did not believe, earlier Phoenician reports that it was possible to sail clear around Africa. In his map, he simply included

Defeated Romans bow down to the barbarian Huns

what he knew—or thought he knew—and left the rest labeled "unknown."

For all its explorations and discoveries, the golden age of Rome was coming to a close. Barbaric nomads from the north—descendants of those same Huns who had once so troubled Chang Ch'ien's Middle Kingdom—swept down into Italy and overran the Roman Empire. By A.D. 476, the last Roman emperor had surrendered to these barbarians. Maps, guidebooks, historic and scientific writings—all that the Greeks and Romans had learned of the world was soon forgotten. India and China became lands only heard of in fairy tales, and for 500 years no one from the Mediterranean lands went exploring. Europe had entered the Dark Ages.

Chapter 8
Journey's End

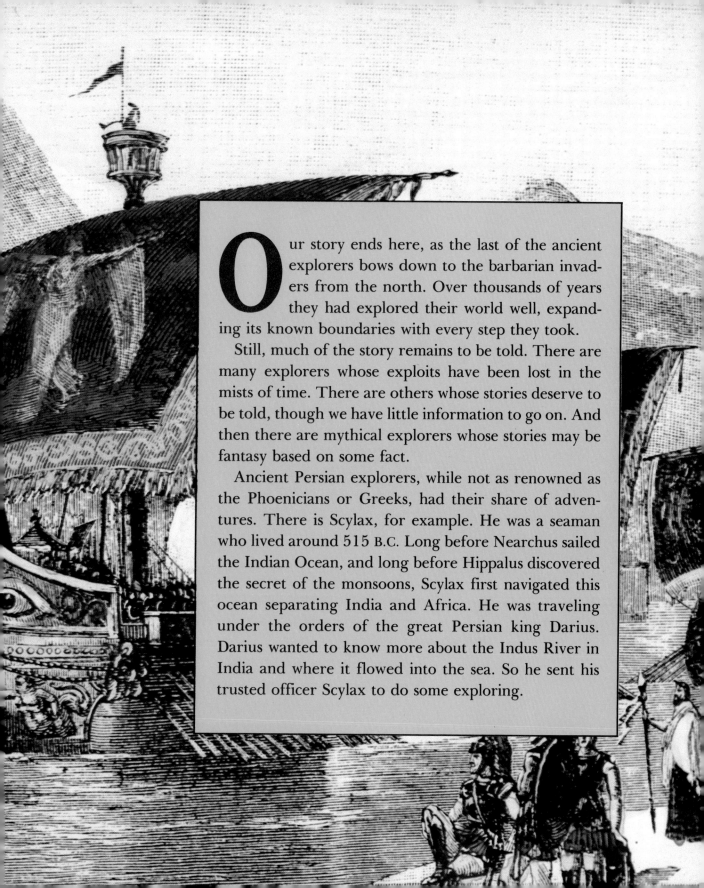

Our story ends here, as the last of the ancient explorers bows down to the barbarian invaders from the north. Over thousands of years they had explored their world well, expanding its known boundaries with every step they took.

Still, much of the story remains to be told. There are many explorers whose exploits have been lost in the mists of time. There are others whose stories deserve to be told, though we have little information to go on. And then there are mythical explorers whose stories may be fantasy based on some fact.

Ancient Persian explorers, while not as renowned as the Phoenicians or Greeks, had their share of adventures. There is Scylax, for example. He was a seaman who lived around 515 B.C. Long before Nearchus sailed the Indian Ocean, and long before Hippalus discovered the secret of the monsoons, Scylax first navigated this ocean separating India and Africa. He was traveling under the orders of the great Persian king Darius. Darius wanted to know more about the Indus River in India and where it flowed into the sea. So he sent his trusted officer Scylax to do some exploring.

Persian king Xerxes retreating to his ships during a battle

Scylax traveled overland to the Indus from Persia. He followed the river to its mouth in the Indian Ocean, and then coasted westward along the shores. He did not sail into the Persian Gulf, which the Persians already knew perfectly well, but instead headed for the Red Sea. Scylax sailed past Arabia—which was new territory for the Persians—and up the Red Sea to present-day Suez. Everywhere he went, he took careful notes to present to his king. It took him two-and-a-half years, but the loyal Scylax eventually completed his mission.

Then there is the unfortunate Sataspes, another Persian. Sataspes lived around 475 B.C., under the rule of the Persian King Xerxes.

Sataspes had gotten into some trouble, and Xerxes threatened to put him to death. When Sataspes's mother pleaded for his life, Xerxes relented—on one condition. Instead of being executed, Sataspes would have to undertake a sea journey to discover whether or not it was possible to sail around Africa. Only then would his life be spared.

Xerxes the Great, king of Persia

Herodotus, known as the Father of History, chronicled the wars between the Persians and Greeks

As the Greek historian Herodotus tells the story, "Xerxes having agreed to these terms, Sataspes came to Egypt and having taken a ship and sailors from the people there sailed for the Pillars of Hercules. Having voyaged out through them he sailed towards the south, but having crossed over much sea in many months, he turned and sailed back to Egypt. And coming thence to King Xerxes' court he told him that at the farthest point of his voyage he sailed by dwarfed men, wearing clothes made from palms. . . . The reason why he did not voyage right round was, he said that the ship was not able to go on farther, but stopped. And so he did not accomplish the task which his mother had laid upon him."

Unfortunately, Xerxes did not believe Sataspes's story, and he had the unsuccessful young sailor put to death anyway.

The Greek story of Jason and his quest for the Golden Fleece was one of the earliest myths of exploration. As legend has it, Jason and his Argonauts set sail around 1250 B.C. Traveling in the good ship Argo of the fifty oars, they went from the Aegean Sea to the Black Sea in search of the mythical Golden Fleece. After having many adventures, they eventually returned home safe and sound.

Jason on his quest for the Golden Fleece

Procession of the Trojan horse in the fabled battle of Troy

Is there any truth to this myth? We know that there were Greeks living along the Black Sea by 750 B.C., and they had to have gotten there somehow. And there are rumors that there really was golden fleece in that part of the country at one time. It was produced by dipping ordinary sheep fleece into gold-bearing streams. Or it could be that the Golden Fleece was a symbol for the riches that Greek traders hoped to find in the Black Sea area. Wherever the truth may lie, it makes a good story!

The travels of the Greek hero Odysseus provide more exciting tales. Odysseus is the hero of the Greek poet Homer's epic verse, the *Odyssey.* In it Odysseus goes to fight the fabled war of Troy. When the war ends,

Odysseus returns home by sea—or he tries to, at any rate. But for ten long years Odysseus is waylaid on his journey. He is blown off course, attacked by sea monsters, and nearly killed a half-dozen times. The places Odysseus goes and the people and monsters he meets are clearly fictional. But his knowledge of seamanship and sea lore is accurate and unmistakable. Did Homer base his story on real stories he had heard about the sea kings of Crete? Was there an element of truth behind all the exaggerated storytelling? We will probably never know for sure. For in the old stories, the possible and the impossible lie side by side. Even the most fantastic happenings may be founded on a grain of truth.

Odysseus defying the frightful, one-eyed Cyclops on his fantastic voyage

The Greek poet Homer reciting one of his epic works

You can see this for yourself in our own story of the explorers of the ancient world. Our information about these ancient discoverers has come down to us in bits and pieces throughout the years.

Some of our information has come from actual journals or reports, written by the explorers themselves and preserved throughout history.

Some information been found in Greek and Roman books of history and geography, either as accurate descriptions about real journeys, or as scattered hints about people and places.

Sometimes we have found physical evidence about ancient explorations—a Minoan gold coin that made its way across the Mediterranean to Italy, for example. We look at such a gold coin and try to figure out how and when it was made, and how and when it got to where it was found.

That coin then becomes just another little piece of the puzzle that we have been putting together for thousands of years.

As you can see, many times our sources of information are not accurate or complete, or even clear. Sometimes we can only make intelligent guesses about what really happened. Sometimes we have to decide between two conflicting versions of the same story. And many times we must use our imaginations to appreciate how truly heroic and resourceful these ancient discoverers really were.

Of course, sometimes our explorers tell us just exactly how extraordinary they were. The Egyptian nobleman Harkhuf was such an explorer. Sent by his Pharaoh around 2300 B.C. to the country of Yam, some 500 miles (805 kilometers) south along the Nile River, Harkhuf had this to say about his trip:

"I was sent to explore a road to this country. I did it in only seven months, and I brought all kinds of gifts from it. I was very greatly praised for it. I brought 300 asses loaded with incense, ebony, grain, panthers, ivory, throw-sticks, and every good product. I was more excellent and vigilant than any count, companion, or caravan conductor, who had been sent to Yam before."

And so too for all our explorers. Whether they were searching for gold or knowledge or military gain, the explorers of the ancient world were, without a doubt, excellent and vigilant beyond compare.

Appendices

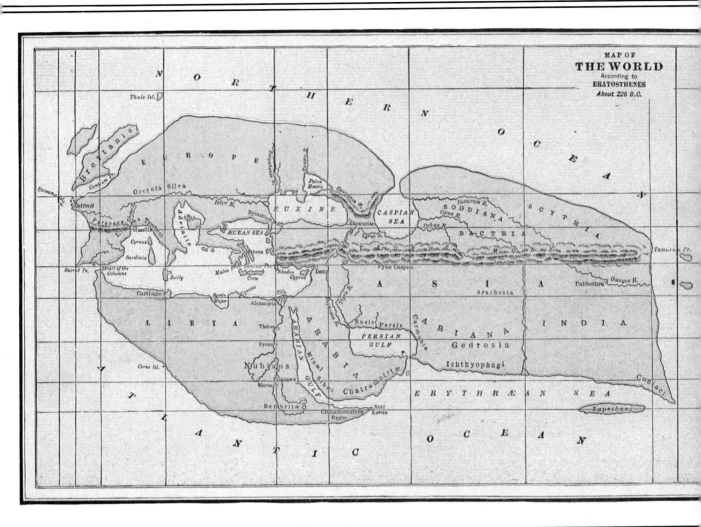

Above: A map of the world according to
Eratosthenes, from about 226 B.C.
Opposite page: Photograph of China taken from the
Landsat 1 satellite. The Great Wall of China, the only
structure made by humans that can be seen from
space, is visible in the upper right and at the bottom
center of the photograph.

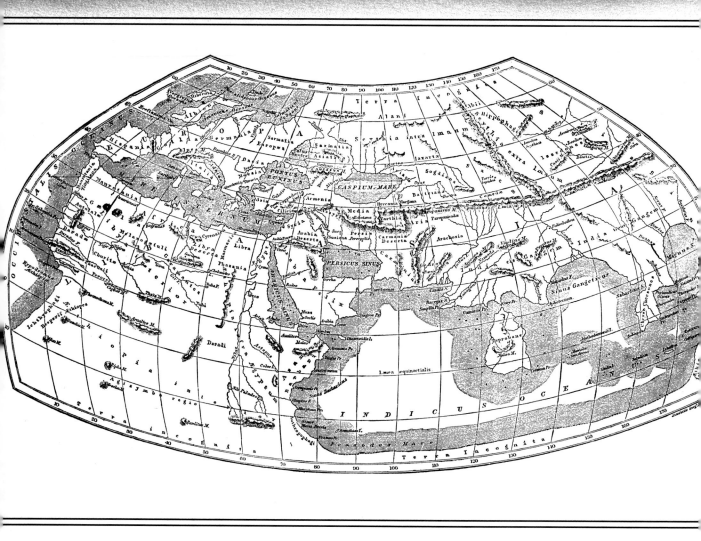

The world according to the geographer Ptolemy

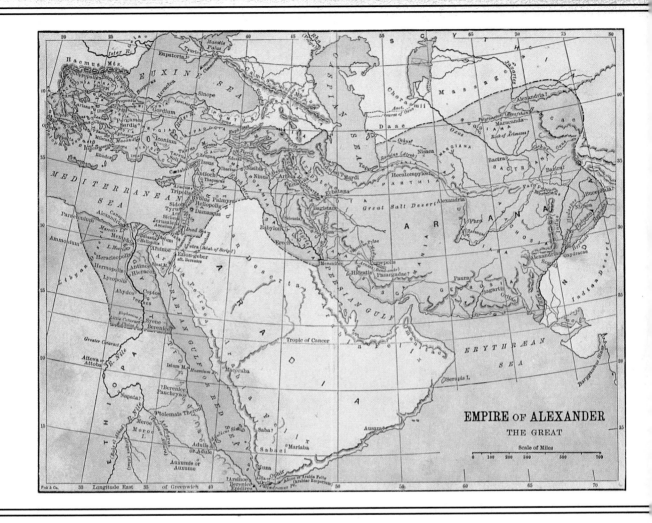

Map showing the empire of Alexander the Great

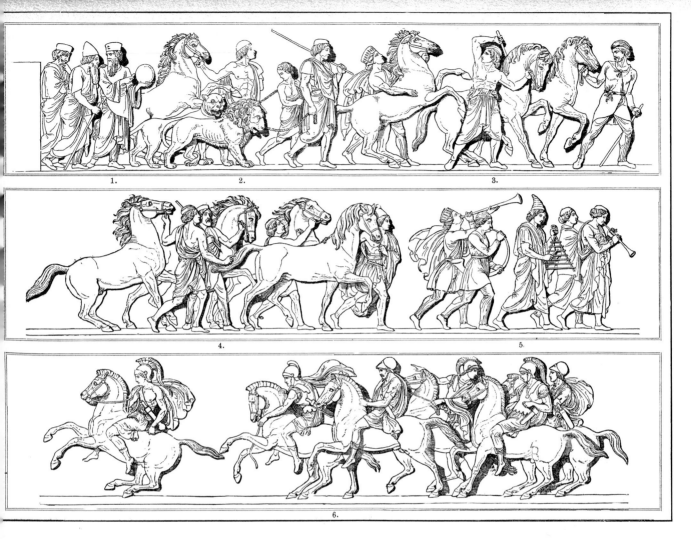

Drawings depicting the travels and campaigns of
Alexander the Great

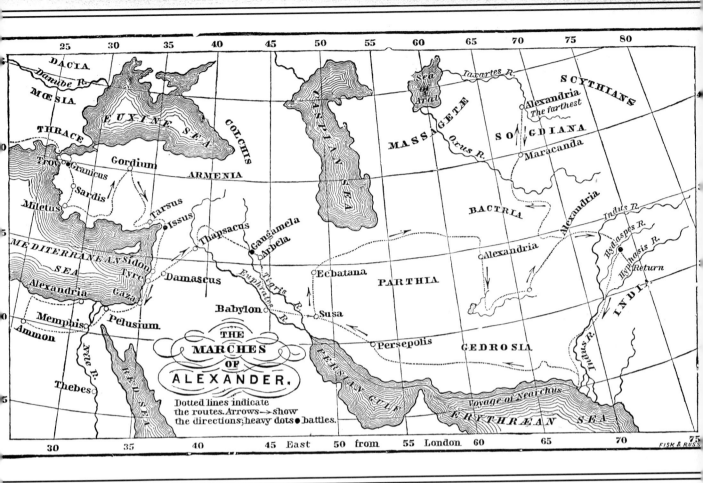

The arrows and dotted lines on this map show the
route Alexander took on his extensive conquest of the
known world.

The earth at the time of Homer, author of the *Odyssey*

Jason slaying a dragon, an etching by Salvator Rosa (1615-1675)

Timeline of Events in Ancient Times

B.C.

c. 9000—Agriculture begins as Middle Eastern peoples begin growing crops and domesticating animals

c. 6500—People of present-day central Mexico begin growing crops

c. 3500—Small settlements grow up in Sumer in the Tigris and Euphrates river valleys

c. 3000—Sumerians develop cuneiform, the first writing system

c. 2900—Egypt's great pyramid is built

c. 2500—The Indus Valley civilization rises in Moen-jo-Daro and Harappa in present-day Pakistan

c. 2500—Minoan civilization begins to flourish on the island of Crete

2300s—Sargon of Akkad defeats Sumerians and rules over all of Mesopotamia, creating the world's first empire

c. 1792–1750—Babylonian civilization flourishes under the rule of Hammurabi

1700s—Code of Hammurabi, one of the world's first codes of law, is devised

1700s—Shang dynasty begins in China's Huang He Valley

c. 1595—Hittites defeat the Babylonians

c. 1503—Hatshepsut, the world's first female ruler, becomes queen of Egypt

c. 1500—Central Asians begin moving into northern India

1500s–1100—Mycenae is the major center of civilization in Greece

c. 1400—Knossos is destroyed, ending the ancient Minoan civilization

c. 1300—Hebrew exodus from Egypt marks the beginnings of Jewish culture and Mosaic law

1020—The Hebrew people found a kingdom in Palestine

800s—Etruscans settle in Italy

c. 800–338—Greek civilization flourishes in Athens, Sparta, Corinth, and Thebes

753—City of Rome is founded

776—First recorded Olympic games are held in Greece

700s—Greek poet Homer composes his epic poems the *Iliad* and the *Odyssey*

c. 550—Cyrus the Great establishes the Persian Empire

524—Gautama Buddha, founder of Buddhism, begins his ministry

509—Romans form a republic after overthrowing their Etruscan rulers

508—Greek democracy begins with the reforms of Cleisthenes

480—Greek civilization is saved from the Persians in the Battle of Salamis

479—The Chinese philosopher Confucius dies; Confucianism begins as his followers spread his teachings

387—Greek philosopher Plato founds his academy

338—Philip II of Macedonia defeats the Greeks

331—Alexander the Great of Macedonia defeats the Persians

323—Death of Alexander the Great

200s—The Septuagint, the Greek version of the Hebrew scriptures, is written

273—Under Asoka's empire, India is united and Buddhism spreads

c. 230—Greek scientist Archimedes develops his inventions

c. 221—Emperor Shih Huang-ti begins building the Great Wall of China

221–206—China's Qin dynasty forms a strong central government

218—Carthaginian general Hannibal crosses the Alps, challenging the Roman republic

202—China's Han dynasty begins its 400-year rule

146—Romans conquer the Greeks

73—Spartacus, a Roman slave, leads a revolt that challenges the Roman social order

49—Julius Caesar begins his rise to power

55–54—Julius Caesar invades Britain

31—Octavius (later Augustus) triumphs at the Battle of Actium, leading to the start of the Roman Empire

27—Augustus becomes the first Roman emperor

A.D.

c. 29—Jesus of Nazareth is crucified, leading to the beginnings of Christianity

70—Romans conquer Jerusalem and destroy the temple, marking the start of the Jewish diaspora

79—Vesuvius volcano erupts, destroying Pompeii

c. 105—In China, Ts'ai Lun invents paper

c. 250—The Mayan civilization begins to flourish in Mexico and Central America

313—Through the Edict of Milan, Roman emperor Constantine grants freedom of worship to Christians

320—India's golden age begins under the Gupta dynasty

360—Huns invade Europe

395—The Roman Empire splits into the eastern, or Byzantine, empire and the western empire

476—Roman Empire falls as Odoacer defeats Roman emperor Romulus Augustulus

Glossary

ancient—Existing in a very early time in history

archaeologist—A scientist who studies the physical remains of long-ago human life

barbarian—A term for wild, primitive, or uncultured peoples

caravan—A group of travelers passing through a region, usually forming a long line

cargo—The goods carried on a ship or other vehicle

century—One hundred years

colony—A settlement of people who have come from one country to live in a new territory

craftsman—A worker who practices an art, skill, or hand craft

ebony—The hard, heavy, black wood of the ebony tree

emperor—Supreme ruler of extensive lands

empire—A widespread territory or group of territories under one ruler

expedition—A journey taken for a specific purpose

historian—A person who studies or writes about history

import—To bring goods into a country

incense—Material that produces a pleasant odor when burned

labyrinth—An arrangement of complex, winding pathways

legend—A popular story from the past that is not necessarily true

mariner—A seaman or sailor

merchant—A buyer and seller of goods

military—Having to do with soldiers, weapons, or wars

monsoon—A periodic high wind in the Indian Ocean and south Asia, often accompanied by heavy rainfall

myrrh—A sharp-smelling, gummy substance that comes from a tree that grows in Arabia and east Africa

myth—A traditional imaginary story by which people explain their beliefs, their view of the world, or happenings in nature

native—Belonging to a certain place by being born or produced there

navigation—The science of getting ships or aircraft from place to place

province—A region or division of a nation

ruins—The remains of a building or city that has collapsed or been destroyed

slave—A person forced to work for another, usually without pay

tax—Money that a government charges on its citizens' personal and business income

tropical—Living or occurring in latitudes just north and south of the equator, the earth's warmest regions

Bibliography

For further reading, see:

Armstrong, Richard. *The Early Mariners*. NY: Frederick Praeger, 1967.

Asimov, Isaac. *The Greeks: A Great Adventure*. Boston: Houghton, Mifflin, 1965.

Barclay, Isobel. *Worlds without End*. NY: Doubleday, 1956.

Colum, Padraic. *The Voyagers*. NY: Macmillan, 1930.

Downey, Glanville. *Stories from Herodotus*. NY: Dutton, 1965.

Duvoisin, Roger. *They Put Out to Sea: The Story of the Map*. NY: Alfred A. Knopf, 1943.

Falls, C. B. *The First 3,000 Years*. NY: Viking, 1960.

Grant, Neil. *Explorers*. Morristown, N.J.: Silver Burdett, 1982.

Hutton, Clarke. *A Picture History of Great Discoveries*. NY: Franklin Watts, 1955.

Parker, John. *Discovery: Developing Views of the Earth*. NY: Charles Scribner's Sons, 1972.

Index

Page numbers in boldface type indicate illustrations.

Picture Identifications for Chapter Opening Spreads

6–7—Sunrise over the Red Sea
18–19—Egypt's pyramids at sunset
32–33—Ras Umm Sid Point and Temple Rock alongside the
       Red Sea on Egypt's Sinai Peninsula
40–41—Remains of a Roman temple at Tyre in present-day
       Lebanon
54–55—Map showing the world according to Herodotus
70–71—The Great Wall of China
86–87—Map of the Roman Empire in the time of Augustus
102–103—Jason and his Argonauts sailing from Corinth

Acknowledgment

For a critical reading of the manuscript, our thanks to John Parker, Ph.D., Curator, James Ford Bell Library, University of Minneapolis, Minneapolis, Minnesota

Picture Acknowledgments

© VIRGINIA GRIMES: 30, 31, 91
HISTORICAL PICTURES SERVICE, CHICAGO: 4, 5, 8, 11, 12, 15, 16, 20, 24, 25 (2 photos), 27, 35 (bottom), 37, 49, 50, 51, 54–55, 57, 58, 60, 63, 70–71, 73, 76, 77, 80, 85, 86–87, 90, 93, 95, 99, 100, 101, 105, 107, 113, 115, 116, 117, 118, 119
NORTH WIND PICTURE ARCHIVES: 2, 9, 14, 17, 23, 42, 43, 45 (2 photos), 52, 53, 56, 59 (2 photos), 61 (2 photos), 62 (bottom), 65, 84, 88, 89, 92, 96, 97, 102–103, 104, 106, 109, 110, 114
PHOTRI: 74, 75, 112
SHOSTAL ASSOCIATES/SUPERSTOCK INTERNATIONAL, INC.: 6–7, 21, 29, 32–33, 35 (top), 36, 38, 39, 40–41, 46
TOM STACK & ASSOCIATES: © M, TIMOTHY O'KEEFE, 18–19; © TOM STACK, 69
TONY STONE WORLDWIDE/CLICK-CHICAGO: © BERLITZ, 34
SUPERSTOCK INTERNATIONAL, INC: 28, 62 (top), 81, 108
COVER ILLUSTRATION BY STEVEN GASTON DOBSON

About the Author

Charnan Simon grew up in Ohio, Georgia, Oregon, and Washington. She holds a B.A. degree in English Literature from Carleton College in Northfield, Minnesota, and an M.A. in English Literature from the University of Chicago. She worked for children's trade book companies after college and became the managing editor of *Cricket* magazine before beginning her career as a free-lance writer. Ms. Simon has written dozens of books and articles for young people and especially likes writing—and reading—history, biography, and fiction of all sorts. She lives in Chicago with her husband and two daughters.